S.M.A.R.T. Pre-K

Stimulating Maturity through Accelerated Readiness Training (S.M.A.R.T.) Pre-K is a program that helps children's brains and bodies get ready to learn. It provides the foundation for the required basic readiness skills, critical for successful learners. The program consists of fun physical activities for developing and/or enhancing large and fine motor skills, balance and coordination, visual efficiency, eye-hand coordination, attention and much more. Once these readiness skills are in place, children have the necessary tools to be able to attend and learn, making them ready for school and to become life-long learners.

A Chance To Grow
Attn: Minnesota Learning Resource Center
1800 Second Street NE
Minneapolis, MN 55418
(612) 789-1236 Fax (612) 706-5555
mlrc@actg.org

www.actg.org

All proceeds from this guide directly benefit A Chance To Grow programs.
A Chance To Grow is an equal opportunity employer.

© 2011, A Chance To Grow, Inc.

Copyright © A Chance To Grow, 1999, Revised 2011

All Rights Reserved

Printed in the United States of America.

No part of this book may be reproduced or utilized in any form or by any means, electronic or mechanical, including photocopying, recording or by any information storage and retrieval system, without prior written permission of the publisher. The only exceptions to the above are texts of 400 words or less, which may be quoted without permission for teaching purposes by instructors trained in the S.M.A.R.T. Pre-K program and only if full credit is given, including the full title, authors' names and publisher's name and address. Inquiries should be addressed to mlrc@actg.org or to A Chance To Grow, Attn: Minnesota Learning Resource Center, 1800 Second Street NE, Minneapolis, MN 55418.

Table of Contents

Dedication 5

Acknowledgements 6

Introduction 8

Understanding the S.M.A.R.T. Principles 11

    S.M.A.R.T. Pre-K 13

    Movement and Learning 19

    Overview of S.M.A.R.T. Pre-K CORE Activities 21

    S.M.A.R.T. Pre-K Roadmap 22

Reflex Activities 23

Balance and Vestibular Activities 31

Gross Motor Activities 45

CORE Vision Activities 61

Putting It All Together 87

    All Through The Day The S.M.A.R.T. Way 89

    S.M.A.R.T. Courses 93

    S.M.A.R.T. Themes 103

Appendices 113

    Appendix A: Letter to Your Families 115

    Appendix B: About A Chance To Grow 117

    Appendix C: S.M.A.R.T. – E.C. Project: Executive Summary 121

Glossary 131

Index 135

This S.M.A.R.T. Pre-K Program Guide
is dedicated to the children and teachers
who shared their knowledge,
their playfulness,
their wisdom
and their time
to assist in its development.

Acknowledgments

The *S.M.A.R.T. Pre-K Program Guides*, in fact, the entire study leading up to creation of the guides, are primarily the result of the work and dedication of two employees of A Chance To Grow, Cheryl Smythe and Leslie Giese. Cheryl coordinated the launching and full five-year study of S.M.A.R.T. Pre-K, involving 20 + Head Start sites, from the development of the program training module aimed at the teacher of the 3 – 5 year old set to the follow-up, onsite mentoring. Leslie worked with Cheryl side-by-side, traveling to the Head Start sites between the Twin Cities metro area and northwestern Minnesota, serving as a mentor and helping to drive the study. This S.M.A.R.T. Pre-K Program Guide is a culmination of what Cheryl and Leslie learned from listening to and observing the Head Start teachers and from their own keen understanding of neurological development. As a result of the work of these two talented, creative and committed women, we feel we have a response to the early childhood community's request for help in getting children ready to learn.

S.M.A.R.T. Pre-K Program Guide Creators

Cheryl Smythe,
MLRC Assistant Director

Leslie Giese,
MLRC Presenter & Mentor

Bob & Kathy DeBoer,
ACTG Co-Founders & Co-Directors

Nancy Farnham,
MLRC Director

Julie Neumann,
M, OTR/L

Cindy Harvey,
MLRC Presenter & Mentor

Kathy Orth,
MLRC Presenter & Mentor

Jodee Kulp,
Program Guide Graphic Designer

The S.M.A.R.T. Pre-K demonstration project was made possible through generous funding provided to A Chance To Grow, which included financial support for an external evaluation. We wish to acknowledge the support of The McKnight Foundation, The Bush Foundation, The Minneapolis Foundation, the Otto Bremer Foundation, the Sheltering Arms Foundation, the Jay and Rose Phillips Foundation, the Fred & Katherine Andersen Foundation, UBS Financial, the Jostens Foundation and the Hugh J. Andersen Foundation.

We also want to recognize the significant contributions made by the extraordinary teachers and administrators of our two S.M.A.R.T. Pre-K partners - MAHUBE Head Start, serving Mahnomen, Hubbard and Becker counties in northwestern Minnesota, and ACCAP Head Start in Anoka and Washington counties of the Twin Cities metro area. The development and creation of S.M.A.R.T. Pre-K would not have been possible without their unfailing commitment to our partnership over the past five years and willingness to open their sites and classrooms to us and share their profound understanding of young children.

MAHUBE

Administrators
Leah Pigatti, Ph.D., Executive Director
Margaret Aho
Joyce Duffney
Michelle Wilkowski

Head Start Teachers
Elissa Braaten
Ky Deblieck
Deb Gilbertson
Edie Kyllonen
Missy Mack
Robin Soyring
Participating Teacher Assistants and Aides

ANOKA-WASHINGTON

Administrators
Jacqueline Cross, Head Start Director
Joyce Kulla
Jan Berqual
Sue Brletich
Kishwar Bayunus
Cindy Rothstein

Head Start Teachers
Cassie Andersen
Jocelyn Bredemus
Kristi Edmonds
Donna Hayes
Priscilla Lalime
Beth Lemke
Freda Schaeffer
Mary Smith
Cindy Sperr
Monica Torgerson
Sandy Urgo
Participating Teacher Assistants and Aides

In addition to our Head Start partners, the school district of Detroit Lakes allowed us to follow the Head Start "graduates" into two of their elementary schools.
Our thanks go to:
Lowell Niklaus, District Curriculum Director
Jerry Hanson, Principal of Roosevelt Elementary
Sanford Nelson, Principal of Rossman Elementary

Introduction

Welcome to the S.M.A.R.T. Pre-K Program Guide – a set of activities and learning readiness exercises that are designed for children in pre-school settings. The S.M.A.R.T. Pre-K Program Guide can be a valuable tool for pre-school teachers who are interested in introducing brain stimulation exercises as an adjunct to the normal pre-school curriculum.

In the past, we assumed that children arrived on the doorsteps of school ready to learn. Unfortunately, that is no longer so – too many children are arriving in kindergarten unprepared to learn and lacking skills needed in order to learn to read, such as listening and speaking skills, visual perception, eye-hand coordination, social interaction patterns, attention to following directions, pencil-paper skills, gross and fine motor skills and self-confidence in the face of challenges. Children entering kindergarten from lower income families and with parents with less education are more likely to be rated as not proficient in language/literacy and mathematical thinking (Department of Education, Minnesota School Readiness Study, 2004).

Over the past decade, there has emerged a growing and strong consensus that early childhood development is a national priority, that early intervention is critical to reducing disparities in language acquisition and learning readiness, and that reducing educational disparities is critical to future economic prosperity and growth. However, while there is strong agreement that more early childhood programming is needed, there is little agreement on "how" to intervene.

The S.M.A.R.T. Program: Since 1985, A Chance To Grow (ACTG) has been committed to the application of brain research, new technology and learning research to overcome the limitations and limited expectations facing children. Initially, ACTG was dedicated to helping children with brain injuries; later, it expanded this focus to include children with learning gaps. Based on ACTG's early clinical work with children with disabilities and developmental delays, a new brain stimulation curriculum was developed to help all children, but especially children who are behind or struggling, develop the readiness for learning, critical for later academic success. This new curriculum was S.M.A.R.T. – Stimulating Maturity through Accelerated Readiness Training. ACTG has spent almost three decades testing and modifying this curriculum for elementary school students and training teachers to introduce brain stimulation exercises into their normal academic routine.

S.M.A.R.T. Pre-K: Although ACTG initially developed S.M.A.R.T. for the early elementary years, it eventually became apparent that it was as, or more, important for the pre-school years. Evidence is mounting regarding the long-term academic and social benefits of early childhood education. And, applying the S.M.A.R.T. program to an even younger age group made sense, since brain development and plasticity at younger ages should make the earlier intervention even more effective as a way to proactively help prepare a child to learn, rather than to remediate once in school.

Getting children ready for school involves more than just rehearsing specific behaviors and skills. Brain stimulation and development are equally important. S.M.A.R.T. Pre-K develops and enhances the physiological readiness skills that children need in order to be ready for and succeed in school. Beginning in 2005, ACTG introduced S.M.A.R.T. Pre-K into two Head Start communities in Minnesota, involving over 20 centers. Head Start centers were deemed good test sites, since all of the children were lower-income and a common set of standards and curriculum were involved. The S.M.A.R.T. Pre-K Program Guide was field-tested at these Head Start centers, half located in the Twin Cities metropolitan area and half in Greater Minnesota. A five-year evaluation of S.M.A.R.T. Pre-K demonstrated that:

- The S.M.A.R.T. Program can be adapted to preschool settings;

- Teachers can learn, accept, and support this new tool;

- Head Start children who received S.M.A.R.T. Pre-K generally performed better on tests of early literacy skills and school readiness than those who did not receive it;

- Head Start children who received S.M.A.R.T. Pre-K entered kindergarten ready to learn and at a level equal to national norms for children at all income levels;

- As Head Start/S.M.A.R.T. Pre-K students progressed through K-2 grades, they continued to learn at levels expected of all students;

- There was no evidence of a "fade" in later grades – the Head Start/S.M.A.R.T. Pre-K students continued to perform at normative levels through Grade 2.

The research findings underscore the importance of brain-related learning and the need to integrate brain stimulation into pre-school settings. It is important to reduce/eliminate learning disparities in the early years so as to prevent negative experiences from interfering with later learning.

This S.M.A.R.T. Pre-K Program Guide is comprehensive, giving teachers a one-stop resource:

- To learn more about the importance of brain development and stimulation as a pre-condition for later learning

- To understand the relationship between brain stimulation exercises and improved brain functioning

- To get suggestions on how to set up a dedicated S.M.A.R.T. Pre-K room or to use existing classrooms

- To learn about the various physical exercises that are the cornerstone of the S.M.A.R.T. Program:

    - Reflex Activities
    - Balance and Vestibular Activities
    - Gross Motor Activities
    - Vision Activities

What is most important to realize about this program is that it can be flexibly applied to a variety of situations—space, time, special needs. And, because the program has been shown to help **all** children in the early years, it can be applied systematically. It is meant to be adapted to your particular classroom setting. Use this Program Guide to suit your needs—as a refresher for what you learned in workshop or as a special guide for the particular activities. It also has a glossary and a set of appendices with supplementary information about S.M.A.R.T. Pre-K.

Understanding the S.M.A.R.T. Principles

We teach you to

"reach the CORE before adding MORE"

to establish solid brain and body connections.

Notes on S.M.A.R.T. CORE:

_____
_____
_____
_____
_____
_____
_____
_____
_____
_____
_____
_____
_____
_____
_____
_____
_____

Read more about the Brain:

Our website:
- www.actg.org

More online resources
- www.brainconnection.com
- www.sfn.org
- www.zerotothree.org/brainwonders
- www.educarer.com/brain.htm
- www.brainy-child.com
- www.preschoolrainbow.org/brain-growth.htm

Books:

Magic Trees of the Mind by Marian Diamond, Ph. D.

Spark: The Revolutionary New Science of Exercise and the Brain
   by John J. Ratey, M.D. and Eric Hagerman

S.M.A.R.T. Pre-K

Stimulating Maturity through Accelerated Readiness Training Pre-K is a program that:

- develops and enhances the physiological readiness skills that children need in order to be ready for and succeed in school
- uses a multi sensory approach to learning
- applies principles of instruction to any curriculum area
- is FUN!

There's been a lot of "buzz" about brain-based learning in the world of education. This is not just another brain-based program. **S.M.A.R.T. Pre-K is a brain stimulation program.** Our approach is developmental, meaning while you may have a classroom of 4 year olds, developmentally their ages may range from 1 to 4 years old. Often times you'll hear a parent or teacher say, "I know she's capable, she's just not trying hard enough." That may be a child who IS capable but developmentally, she's just not yet able to take in and process information efficiently.

> **S.M.A.R.T. Pre-K provides brain stimulating activities to help bring children up to or beyond their age level and prepare them to learn prior to entering elementary school.**

S.M.A.R.T. stands for

Stimulating

Maturity through

Accelerated

Readiness

Training

 Notes to the Reader

- Throughout the *S.M.A.R.T. Pre-K Program Guide*, female pronouns have been used for the child for consistency purposes only.

- It is assumed you, and/or another adult, will monitor the children during all of these activities to ensure quality.

© 2011, A Chance To Grow, Inc.

Here are some brain basics:

- Our brains learn by seeing, hearing and touching things many, many, many times.

- Our brains also learn through intense stimulation.

- Our brains learn over time.

Stimulating

We use the S.M.A.R.T. concepts—Stimulating, Maturity, Accelerated, Readiness and Training—to help you understand the connection between learning and the brain.

Let's first look at **Stimulating.** Our brains learn by seeing, hearing and touching things many, many, many times. One of the first words a baby learns to say is "No!" It's not a miracle that is one of their first words. They hear the word, "No!" many, many times in the first year or so of life. It is truly a learned process, based on the experience of hearing "NO!" so frequently.

If you've studied physiology, you've likely heard the following three concepts:

1. Frequency
2. Intensity
3. Duration

These apply to brain stimulation as well.

Frequency In the S.M.A.R.T. Pre-K program, we do activities many times, or with increased frequency. **We give children MANY exposures or "inputs" to concepts.** Most curricula give a few exposures and then go right into quizzing or testing mode. We want you to really think of your instruction as INPUT instruction, or increasing the frequency of the INPUTs to the brain.

Intensity Our brains also learn through intense stimulation. Intensity can be how big, how bright, how hard, how fast, how exciting, etc. Think in terms of kicking your curriculum up a notch or two!

Duration is another variable we use to teach children. We keep the stimulation going throughout the entire year. Think of duration as running a marathon versus a sprint. We are in it for the "long haul" with children.

Maturity

Now, let's look at **Maturity,** as in maturing systems within the brain and body so that both are ready to learn. Brain stimulation through the S.M.A.R.T. Pre-K program aims to mature sensory pathways of vision, auditory and tactile/kinesthetic and we "measure" the maturation through the motor pathways of mobility, language and manual. It works like this; you receive stimulus or INPUT through the sensory pathways. The brain processes the information and then you have motor responses or OUTPUT through the motor pathways.

Due to Readiness Skill Deficits, the input into some children is not clear and/or consistent and there appear to be "gaps" in learning. Therefore, the output is the same and the same "gaps" appear. These children cannot perform at their natural intelligence, even though they are trying as hard as they can.

> *Brain stimulation through the S.M.A.R.T. Pre-K program aims to mature sensory pathways of vision, auditory and tactile/kinesthetic.*

Acceleration

> Our hope as educators is to help the messages travel quickly and efficiently.
>
> We want to accelerate both the speed and efficiency of each message.
>
> **First** by increasing the paths by which the message can travel.
>
> **Second** by increasing the speed at which the message can travel.
>
> One neuron can connect with between two and twenty thousand other neurons.

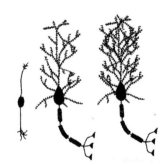

Newborn dendritte   Toddler dendritte   Adult dendritte

Acceleration, now here is where we take education to a cellular level! A brain cell is called a neuron and we all have 10 billion + neurons. Neurons are unique in that they communicate with each other. Neurons are messengers. Each neuron has an axon that transmits an electrical-chemical charge. The electrical charge, once it has developed sufficient potency, jumps the synaptic cleft/gap by way of chemicals called neurotransmitters. Then the electrical charge is received by the dendrites of a second neuron. Our hope as educators is to help the messages to travel quickly and efficiently. We want to accelerate both the speed and efficiency of the neuron's message!

That happens in two ways, **first by increasing the paths** by which the message can travel and **second by increasing the speed** at which the message travels. Novel stimulation causes the neurons to grow branches called dendrites and connect to other cells. More connections make more options and therefore more efficient travel. Each dendrite can connect with between 2 and 20,000 other dendrites. Now that is a lot of options for the brain to take when sending a message!

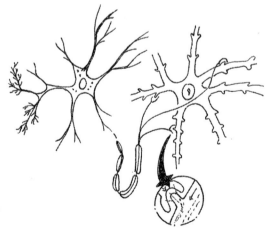

Myelin is a fatty layered tissue that sheathes the axon of each neuron. This sheath around the axon acts like a conduit in an electrical system, ensuring that messages sent by axons move quickly and are not lost en route. Picture a regular extension cord versus the thick, heavy-duty orange extension cord. The thicker the insulation on the cord, the higher the rating and capability it has. The thicker the myelin on the axon, the faster the message can be transmitted. Many layers allows for efficient conduction of the electrical impulse down the axon. The more positive stimulation the brain receives, the more myelin is produced.

Readiness

To explain **Readiness**, it is important that you understand the functions of two areas of the brain. The first is the Brain Stem (here we mean Pons, Medulla and Cerebellum), which controls the coordination of all unconscious motor activity. It is the area in charge of automatic function and is the foundation for readiness skills.

Here are some examples of these skills:

- Eyes moving smoothly together across a page
- A sense of balance that allows a child to sit upright in a chair
- Ability to differentiate between similar sounds

It is crucial that these skills are automatic or unconscious when we are learning. If they are not unconscious, then they must be conscious. This is important, because if the skills are done consciously, then the Cortex of the brain is involved. The Cortex can do one thing at a time. If the Brain Stem is not doing its work (automatic function), then the Cortex can concentrate to make the eyes move smoothly across a page of text and a student may appear to be able to read. But, the ROLE of the Cortex in reading is to do the comprehension. If the Cortex is involved or "taken up" with the eye movements, then it is no longer available for the comprehension because it can only do one job. The result or results are things educators see every day when teaching children.

Children who:
- **Only seem to be able to follow one step in a list of directions**
- **Seem to have learned a skill in isolation, but cannot transfer it**
- **Can read a text but cannot remember what they just read**

With S.M.A.R.T. Pre-K, we aim to have the foundation skills in place, so the BRAIN STEM can perform automatic functions and the CORTEX can perform higher functioning work such as analysis and comprehension!

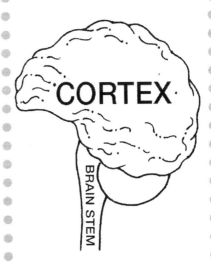

With S.M.A.R.T. Pre-K, we aim to have the foundation skills in place, so the BRAIN STEM can perform automatic functions and the CORTEX can perform higher functioning work such as analysis and comprehension!

Using the principles of

Stimulation,

Maturity,

Acceleration and

Readiness

Trains the brain and body to be ready to learn.

Training

Finally, we come to **Training**. In the S.M.A.R.T. Pre-K program children do many activities which TRAIN or encourage the brain to use both hemispheres at the same time. Despite the split, the two hemispheres of the brain communicate with each other through a thick tract of white nerve fibers called the Corpus Callosum. It connects the two hemispheres and transfers important information from one side to the other.

We want to train the two hemispheres to communicate because using both sides of the brain is very important when learning how to read and when expressing feelings and thoughts…

- Right hemisphere controls feelings and thoughts
- Left hemisphere controls language
- We use both sides when we talk about how we feel

Training is also using all of these principles together; Stimulation, Maturity, Acceleration and Readiness to Train the brain. We do this through a series of specific activities, which integrate into your existing curriculum, to make the brains and bodies of your children ready so they can learn.

Movement and Learning

Most Pre-K programs include some time during the day for gross motor activities. As educators, we may think this time helps children "get the wiggles out," but something more important is happening with all of this movement.

Movement influences the ability to concentrate in a classroom and to learn to read and write.

Developmentally, movement plays a major role in understanding our bodies. Belly crawling, creeping on hands and knees, rolling, climbing, pushing and pulling are just a few of the movements we draw from in the S.M.A.R.T. Pre-K program. We aim to mature Reflexes, Balance, Vestibular, Gross and Fine Motor, Proprioception, Bilateral Coordination, Vision and Auditory systems. When children engage in the purposeful movements of the S.M.A.R.T. Pre-K program, they mature their bodies and brains.

Children with mature bodies and brains are more capable of sitting still and remaining seated in their chairs. They also have an understanding of how much or how little force should be used when turning pages in a book or using writing utensils. These skills do not happen automatically, or mature as the pages of the calendar turns. Immature development can look like children who have to move around a lot, or those who use too much force or appear not to be paying attention.

Additionally, it takes great endurance by these same body systems to be able to sit still at a desk and do work quietly. **Essentially, our bodies NEED to move in order to learn HOW to be still.** We are not born with this skill, it is learned. We build up the endurance by having a significant amount of movement and therefore stimulation to brain and body systems. So, plan for lots of purposeful movement breaks during your day. **Young children need to move; the movement helps them know where their bodies are. Being still does not.** If you plan for movement (rather than just letting it happen when it will), then it won't feel like a disruption, but more like a part of your day!

Movement influences the ability to concentrate in a classroom and to learn to read and write.

Essentially, our bodies NEED to move in order to learn HOW to be still.

Knowing this, purposeful movement is an important strategy we use. The body is designed to move. Research shows that purposeful, specific and systematic physical movement can affect the brain in a very positive and dramatic way.

Physical activity helps create an optimal learning condition for the brain by:

- **Increasing** dendrite branching and creating more connections. More connections to other cells increase the complex combinations of cells to receive and transmit information.

- **Stimulating** the brain to produce myelin and faster connections. The myelin sheath around the transmitting axon allows the impulses to travel more quickly.

- **Feeding** the brain glucose and oxygen, which is brain food. When we exercise, more oxygen and glucose (which is carried in our blood) gets to the brain.

MOVEMENT anchors learning!

If movement anchors learning, we need to put more movement into learning. Special educators, physical educators, occupational and physical therapists have long recognized this crucial connection between physical movement and learning. Thinking and learning are not all in our head. On the contrary, the body plays an integral part in our intellectual processes. Research shows that there is a connection between activity and levels of alertness, mental function and learning. With this in mind, it's important that educators continue to allow and promote children having physical movement throughout their day, every day!

> *Research shows that purposeful, specific and systematic physical movement can affect the brain in a very positive and dramatic way.*

Overview of S.M.A.R.T. Pre-K CORE Activities

Reflex Activities

Superman	Popcorn

Balance and Vestibular Activities

Pencil Rolls	Flamingos
Helicopter Spins	Hopscotch
Stable Table	Rebounder
Balance Beam	

Gross Motor Activities

Alligator Crawl	Overhead Ladder
Slap Track	Cross Patterning
Free Creep	

CORE Vision Activities

Tactile Trackers	Swinging Ball
Flower Power	Loop de Loos
Driver's Ed	Overs and Unders
Magic Erasers	Basic Vision
Thumbs Up	Near/Far Focus

Complete CORE before adding MORE!

"Children who are moving around your classroom are showing they need more movement to learn how to be still."

© 2011, A Chance To Grow, Inc.

S.M.A.R.T. Pre-K Guide Roadmap

TEACHER TOOLBOX
- Tells you the supplies you will need to perform the activities.

 S.M.A.R.T. PRE-K CORE ACTIVITY
This is a S.M.A.R.T. Pre-K CORE Activity. Each activity takes just a few minutes to do. They can be done individually throughout the day and/or in combination for a goal of: 20 minutes, every day, all year through. We help you lay that out in the "Putting It All Together" section on page 87.

 **SAFETY FIRST** Before you proceed with an activity.

⚠ Please read these sections—this is important information in the development of the children you serve.

Note: ✏ ☐ Tips to help you support the children you are teaching.

That's one S.M.A.R.T. Teacher!
 When you see the apple bullet look for a great tip or idea from S.M.A.R.T. teachers.

♥ **Fun** ♥
Enhance your program.

LEARNING Stage 1
"I'm Learning"
Things you will see if the **skill is emerging**.

WORKING Stage 2
"Still Working"
Things you will see as the **skill develops**.

GOT IT! Stage 3
"I've got it!"
Things you will see when the **skill is mature**.

☺ **Start where the child is at.** Children develop at different rates. Often, chronological and developmental ages are not the same. Some children will have emerging skills, some are further along in developing the skill and others will have the skill already in place. All children, even those who have the skill, benefit from doing S.M.A.R.T. Pre-K activities because they strengthen connections in the brain and body. When working with a group of 3, 4 and 5 year olds you will see children in all three stages.

Reflex Activities

"Reflexes are built-in 'PRE-FABRICATED' movement responses that we are born with. All reflexes are involuntary…and are available as long as they serve their purpose: Their purpose is to provide a learning experience for the brain."

– Athena Oden, Physical Therapist
Author of Ready Bodies, Learning Minds

1. Superman
2. Popcorn

Notes on Reflexes:

_____
_____
_____
_____
_____
_____
_____
_____
_____
_____
_____
_____
_____
_____
_____

Read more about Reflexes:

- www.readybodies.com
- www.masgutovamethod.com
- www.mamabebe.org
- www.brainandbehaviour.ie
- www.keepkidshealthy.com/newborn/newborn_reflexes.html

Reflexes

Superman

Tonic Labyrinthine Reflex (TLR) in prone Integration

TEACHER TOOLBOX
- Open floor space

Note: ✏️
- ☐ Start with holding for 5 seconds.
- ☐ Then after 1 - 2 weeks, start holding for 10 seconds.
- ☐ After another 1 - 2 weeks start holding for 15 seconds.
- ☐ Finally, have the children hold for 20 seconds.

How to do it

1. Teacher model, if possible, or use a child to model.

2. Lying flat on their stomachs, have the children raise their chin off of the floor, bring their extended arms overhead close to the ears and lift their straightened legs off the floor.

3. Their bodies should be taut, only touching the floor at the midriff.

4. Ask the children to hold this position for 20 seconds.
   Repeat 3 times.

⚠️ They should be able to maintain the position with their arms forward and with their legs fully extended.

There should be no rocking, rolling or waving of arms.

That's one S.M.A.R.T. Teacher!

🍎 **Monica in Coon Rapids** uses music as an auditory cue! She plays the Superman theme song for 5 seconds at first and builds up to 20 seconds. Both she and her assistant monitor the positioning.

🍎 **Ky in Park Rapids** after she teaches "Superkids" to her class, she gets down onto the floor and does it right along with them! Her assistant teacher monitors the positioning.

 Fun

- ♥ Use **"Fly"** when telling the child to get into the Superman position.
- ♥ Use **"Land"** when it is time to rest.

Ready Bodies, Learning Minds,
Athena Oden, P.T., ©2004

Reflexes

What does it do?

The repetition of a proper movement pattern will help integrate the reflex and therefore help eliminate an obligatory movement pattern and its consequences. Assist the children and train them to perform the exercise correctly until they can do it independently and without difficulty.

When to do exercises.

These exercises can be done any time of day, once a day or several times a day. There is not a prescriptive rate, but the rule of thumb is "the more, the better."

Note:

- ☐ Teaching the children to complete this exercise can be done in several steps depending on the level of competency.
- ☐ Along each step of this process, you may assist a child in assuming the position, holding it momentarily, and then asking the child to hold it momentarily. The child with difficulty will build the movement faster this way than by asking her to create the movement herself, or initiate it from the starting position of lying on the floor.

WORKING Stage 2

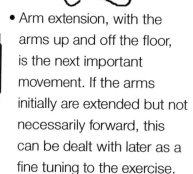

- Arm extension, with the arms up and off the floor, is the next important movement. If the arms initially are extended but not necessarily forward, this can be dealt with later as a fine tuning to the exercise.
- Leg extension is the next step in learning the exercise. If a child is not getting her legs off the floor or is bending her knees, you will need to let her feel the movement by holding her legs in place for her. Holding the legs up under the thighs and knees will give the child tactile feedback about her position in space.

LEARNING Stage 1

- The initial movement of head up and trunk raised off the floor is usually not difficult for children this age. If it is, start this movement with your assistance if necessary.

GOT IT! Stage 3

- The children must be able to assume this position (head/arms/legs up all at once) quickly and automatically. Therefore, an auditory stimulus, such as clapping, is used as a cue for the children to rise quickly into this position.
- They should be able to maintain the position with their arms forward and with their legs fully extended.

☺ **Start where the child is at.** For example, if a child is at Stage 2, begin there and progress forward. For more information see page 22.

 Reflexes

Ready Bodies, Learning Minds, Athena Oden, P.T., ©2004

Popcorn

Tonic Labyrinthine Reflex (TLR) in supine Integration

TEACHER TOOLBOX
- Open floor space

Note:
- ☐ Start with holding for 5 seconds.
- ☐ Then after 1 - 2 weeks, start holding for 10 seconds.
- ☐ After another 1 - 2 weeks start holding for 15 seconds.
- ☐ Finally, have the children hold for 20 seconds.

How to do it

1. Teacher model, if possible, or use a child to model.

2. With the children lying flat on their backs, ask them to bring their knees to their chests, wrapping their arms around their legs.

3. They should then lift their heads, trying to keep their eyes close to their knees.

4. Ask the children to hold this position for 20 seconds. **Repeat 3 times.**

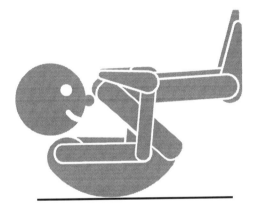

♥ More Fun ♥

♥ Use **"Kernel Up"** when telling the children to get into the Popcorn position.

♥ You can tell the children to **"park your nose in the garage,"** the space between their knees.

♥ Fun Stuff ♥

♥ For a fun release movement, they may POP out with their body straight and taut, feet together and arms moving above their head to a flat position on the floor = "Popcorn."

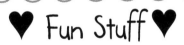

Ready Bodies, Learning Minds,
Athena Oden, P.T., ©2004

Reflexes

⚠️ The children should maintain the position in a calm, relaxed manner. The children should not rock or roll on their back.

- They should be resting their weight on the midback. It is not appropriate to rise to a position of weight on the hips as they reach for and hold their legs.

- It is also inappropriate to roll back to weight-bearing on the shoulders.

- The position of the head is very important. Since the position of the labyrinths control this reflex, the neck should always be flexed forward. You may have to position the head for a child with the eyes close to the knees and hold it momentarily to teach this position. This may have to be done numerous times for the child to begin to assume the neck flexion on their own.

That's one S.M.A.R.T. Teacher!

🍎 **Kristi in Anoka** motivates her children by adding some "spice" to the activity! When her children do a great job, she tells them *"You did that one so well, I think I'll add some butter to the popcorn!"* Kristi has also been known to add salt, cheese and caramel!

🍎 **Monica in Coon Rapids** does Popcorn right after group time! She simply has her children lay back right where they were sitting and they begin. It truly adds just one minute of time because they are already in place on the floor.

🍎 **Ky in Park Rapids** after she teaches Popcorn to her class, she gets down onto the floor and does it right along with them! Her assistant teacher monitors the positioning.

Reflexes

Ready Bodies, Learning Minds,
Athena Oden, P.T., ©2004

What does it do?

The repetition of a proper movement pattern will help integrate the reflex and therefore help eliminate an obligatory movement pattern and its consequences. Assist the children and train them to perform the exercise correctly until they can do it independently and without difficulty.

Note: ✏️
- As noted in the previous discussion of the TLR prone exercise, this exercise should be taught in incremental stages if necessary.

When to do exercises.

These exercises can be done any time of day, once a day or several times a day. There is not a prescriptive rate, but the rule of thumb is "the more, the better."

LEARNING Stage 1

- The child may need help flexing her knees to her chest and learning how to hold them. She should not be holding her clothes, and it is best if the ankles are not crossed.

WORKING Stage 2

- The position of the head is very important. Since the position of the labyrinths control this reflex, the neck should always be flexed forward. You may have to position the head for the child with the eyes close to the knees and hold it momentarily to teach this position. This may have to be done numerous times for the child to begin to assume the neck flexion on her own.

GOT IT! Stage 3

- The children must be able to assume this position (head/arms/legs up all at once) quickly and automatically. Therefore, an auditory stimulus, such as clapping, is used as a cue for the children to rise quickly into this position.
- They should be able to maintain the position with their arms, legs and neck legs fully flexed.

☺ **Start where the child is at.** For example, if a child is at Stage 2, begin there and progress forward. For more information see page 22.

Ready Bodies, Learning Minds,
Athena Oden, P.T., ©2004

Reflexes

Reflexes

Balance and Vestibular Activities

"The Vestibular System is the unifying system... activity in the Vestibular System provides a framework for the other aspects of our experiences."

– Jean Ayres, Ph.D., OTR
Pioneer in the field of Sensory Integration

1. Pencil Rolls
2. Helicopter Spins
3. Stable Table
4. Flamingos
5. Balance Beam
6. Hopscotch
7. Rebounder

Notes on Balance and Vestibular:

_____
_____
_____
_____
_____
_____
_____
_____
_____
_____
_____
_____
_____
_____
_____
_____
_____

Read more about Balance and Vestibular:

- www.developmentaldelay.net/page.cfm/14
- www.livestrong.com/article/215788-vestibular-exercises-for-children/
- www.ehow.com/info_7982798_vestibular-balance-activities-children.html
- www.braintraining.com/vestibular.htm

Catalogs

- www.achievement-products.com

Balance and Vestibular

Pencil Rolls

To develop proprioception and low-level vestibular and visual skills.

TEACHER TOOLBOX
- Open floor space of 15 - 18 feet
  We recommend you tape off a line with painter's tape.
  OR
- (2) 4 x 8 mats = 16 feet

How to do it

This activity is written as individual use for safety.
It is intended to be used in a S.M.A.R.T. Course where all children participate.

1. Teacher model, if possible, or use a child to model.

2. Have the child lie flat on one end of the mat or rolling area.

3. Have the child lie on the mat with:
   - Arms and hand extended overhead
   - Palms of the hands and fingers touching
   - Legs straight and together
   - Toes pointed

*Remember to **encourage the children** to use their hips like wheels as they roll.*

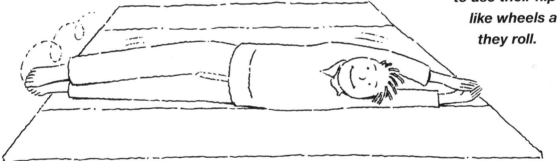

4. Have the child roll down the length, moving in a straight line as quickly as tolerated by the child.

5. As skill continues to increase, have the child increase speed.

⚠ Let the child in front roll out of the way, at least 8 feet, before the next child begins. Use a taped line to help the children self-monitor. *"When the child in front of you gets to the tape it is safe for you to go."*

If using a taped line on the floor, the child aligns her shoulder with the line in an effort to roll straight.

Balance and Vestibular

© 2011, A Chance To Grow, Inc.

When using Pencil Rolling in a S.M.A.R.T. Space Obstacle Course:

- Be sure to leave space between the children for safety.
- If short on space, have the child roll down and back on the mat or length of floor space.

That's one S.M.A.R.T. Teacher!

 Robin in Detroit Lakes has her children roll while on field trips! While at the Apple Orchard and waiting for the bus to pull up, her children roll down a hill or across a grassy area.

 Ky in Park Rapids puts something under one of the mats to create a bump for the children to roll over!

♥ Fun Stuff ♥

- ♥ Have the children hold an object (toy, soft ball, stuffed animal) above their heads while they roll.
- ♥ Have the children roll down the hall.
- ♥ Have the children roll down a hill or across a grassy area.
- ♥ Have the children pretend they are a crayon rolling across the table, *"Pick your favorite color!"*
- ♥ Have children pretend they are a hotdog and roll fast because the "grill" is hot! *"Stay on the mat."* If they roll off the "grill" they will have to be fed to the dog because the hotdog got dirty.
- ♥ This activity can be used in connection with Fire Safety, *"Stop, Drop and Roll."*

*Roll, roll, roll around
as fast as you can go
Round and round and
round and round
helping you to grow*

— Sung to Row Row Row Your Boat

LEARNING Stage 1

- The child may need assistance at first with rolling over and keeping her arms and legs straight.

WORKING Stage 2

- The children may not roll straight.
- The child may roll slower, as tolerated by the child. With enough exposure this will mature.

GOT IT! Stage 3

- The children can stay straight and roll quickly.

☺ **Start where the child is at.** For example, if a child is at Stage 2, begin there and progress forward. For more information see page 22.

Balance and Vestibular

Helicopter Spins

TEACHER TOOLBOX
- Open floor space
- CD player
- Various selections of music

To develop basic balance and vestibular skills.

How to do it

1. Teacher model, if possible, or use a child to model.

2. Have the children spread out in the room and place their arms out straight from their shoulders like a "T."

 Safety check:

3. Have the children check their space to make sure they have enough room to spin safely.

4. Turn the music on and have the children spin for 15 seconds.

5. Have the children stop and stand for 15 seconds. The children should NOT use anything to help them with balance when they stop after each spin.

6. Repeat the start and stop (30 seconds) sequence 10 times throughout the day for a total of 5 minutes daily.

 As children are able to successfully stop and hold the position in balance, they may hold their arms by their sides rather than in the "T." Children should not spin with hands in their pockets.

Children should NOT use anything to help them with balance when they stop after each spin. If a child has difficulty regaining balance initially, she should spread her feet apart to extend the base of balance.

Spinning is cumulative. Example: Mix and match times – 3 spins at beginning of day, 4 spins before playground and 3 spins after center time.

Balance and Vestibular

© 2011, A Chance To Grow, Inc.

That's one S.M.A.R.T. Teacher!

- **Missy in Frazee** uses streamers with spinning! Her children really like to feel the streamers when they spin around.

- **Leslie in Drexel** has her children spin like blenders. *"Let's add three strawberries."* The children take off pretend tops, add three and push their noses to start their blenders.

♥ Fun ♥

- ♥ Have the children pretend they are helicopters taking off for a trip to Minneapolis, New York, Dallas, Knoxville, etc.
- ♥ Have the children pretend they are blenders making milk shakes, adding ice cream, flavors, etc.
- ♥ Have the children pretend they are twirling snowflakes, twisting tornados, pirouetting ballerinas or rotating ice skaters.
- ♥ Spin with scarves and streamers in their hands.

About the Music

- The music should be loud but not so loud that it is uncomfortable. Your voice should be able to be heard above the music.
- The music should be upbeat and something that children do not listen to regularly. Use music like island, ethnic, classical, parade and march music. A variety of music is stimulating.
- The music can be played continuously or turned off and on as a command of start and stop.

LEARNING Stage 1

- A child may experience discomfort when spinning. She could spin slower, keep her eyes open and/or reduce the number or duration of spins.
- Initially it may be necessary to spin and stop for two to three minutes or four to six spins.

WORKING Stage 2

- The child may spin slowly and/or get very dizzy when spinning.
- The child may be very wobbly when stopping. With enough exposure, this will mature.

GOT IT! Stage 3

- The children can spin quickly and stop with complete balance for the full duration of the activity.

☺ **Start where the child is at.** For example, if a child is at Stage 2, begin there and progress forward. For more information see page 22.

Balance and Vestibular

Stable Table

To improve body concept and develop better balance and control, both stationary and in movement.

TEACHER TOOLBOX
- Open floor space

How to do it

The goal for all of the following steps is to maintain balance for 10 seconds.

1. Teacher model, if possible, or use a child to model.

2. Have the children get into the Stable Table position:
   - Hands and knees on floor
   - Hands directly under shoulders
   - Hands flat on the floor and fingers pointed straight ahead
   - Knees directly under the hips
   - Feet resting on the floor directly behind the hips
   - Head is looking straight forward
   - Back is flat

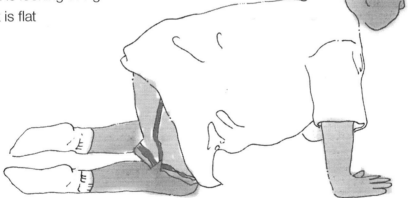

3. When the children are able to successfully hold the Stable Table position in balance without moving other parts of the body, wobbling or falling over, they can move to the next step in the progression listed on the next page.

- **♥ Play Musical Tables** Have the children start in the Stable Table position. Turn on music and have the children creep (see Free Creep Activity on page 55) around the room. Turn the music off and have the children stop in the Stable Table position.

Balance and Vestibular

© 2011, A Chance To Grow, Inc.

These steps are developmentally arranged.
Master each step reasonably well before moving to the next step in the progression.

The next step ...

Have the children start in the Stable Table position.

- The children raise their right hand off the floor and hold it out in front of them.
- The children should look straight ahead with their eyes open.
- Their backs should be flat and, when they lift their arms, no other part of their bodies should move out of the starting position.
- The children must hold this position for 10 seconds.

Next steps of progression:

(1) Raising the left hand
(2) Raising the right leg
(3) Raising the left leg
(4) Raising the left arm and right leg
(5) Raising the right arm and left leg

 Fun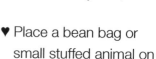

- Place a bean bag or small stuffed animal on the middle of the back. *"Keep the zebra on your table."*
- Place a piece of food from the play kitchen on the middle of the back.
- While holding the Stable Table position do Eye Movement Activities such as Flower Power (page 66).

LEARNING Stage 1
- The child may not be able to hold the position with complete balance.

WORKING Stage 2
- The child may be able to hold the position for 5 seconds.

GOT IT! Stage 3
- The children are able to hold the position with complete balance for 10 seconds.

☺ **Start where the child is at.** For example, if a child is at Stage 2, begin there and progress forward. For more information see page 22.

 Balance and Vestibular

Flamingos

To improve body concept and develop better balance and control, both stationary and in movement.

TEACHER TOOLBOX
- Open floor space

How to do it

The goal for all of the following steps is to maintain balance for 10 seconds.

1. Teacher model, if possible, or use a child to model.

2. Have the children stand on their tiptoes with eyes open.

3. When children are able to successfully hold this position in balance without moving other parts of their bodies, wobbling or falling over, they can move to the next step in progression listed below.

Next steps of progression:

(1) Stand on one foot with eyes open
(2) Stand on the other foot with eyes open
(3) Stand on tiptoes with eyes closed
(4) Stand on one foot with eyes closed
(5) Stand on the other foot with eyes closed

⚠ These steps are developmentally arranged. Master each step reasonably well before moving to the next step in the progression.

LEARNING Stage 1
- The child may not be able to hold the position with complete balance.

WORKING Stage 2
- The child may be able to hold the position for 5 seconds.

GOT IT! Stage 3
- The children are able to hold the position with complete balance for 10 seconds.

☺ **Start where the child is at.** For example, if a child is at Stage 2, begin there and progress forward. For more information see page 22.

Balance and Vestibular

© 2011, A Chance To Grow, Inc.

Balance Beam

To develop balance skills.

TEACHER TOOLBOX
- Balance Beam

OR
- Painter's tape

OR
- (2 - 3) yardsticks Velcroed to the floor

AND
- Bean bags/balls (optional)

How to do it

This activity is written as individual use for safety. **It is intended to be used in a S.M.A.R.T. Course where all children participate.**

1. Teacher model, if possible, or use a child to model.

2. Have the child walk forward, heel-to-toe with eyes open across the beam. The child should move slowly across the beam. *"Slow is good!"*

3. When the child is able to walk completely across the balance beam, without any wobbling or falling off, she may move to the next steps in the progression listed below.

Next steps of progression:
(1) Walk forward, heel-to-toe with eyes open with a bean bag balanced on her head
(2) Walk forward, heel-to-toe with eyes open while tossing a bean bag or ball into a basket placed on the floor at the end of the beam
(3) Walk backwards, heel-to-toe with eyes open across the beam

⚠ For all of the balance beam activities the children must move SLOWLY, moving too quickly across the beam does not challenge the balance system.

Initially for balance, the children may need to place their arms out straight from the shoulders like a "T." If additional assistance is needed, you may place a finger in the middle of a child's back. **Holding the child's hand does not challenge the balance system.**

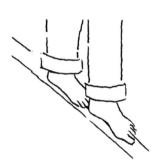

That's one S.M.A.R.T. Teacher!

 Mary in Forest Lake gets down onto the floor and helps each child learn the right way to walk heel-to-toe in the beginning of the year! She places each foot if necessary. Her children "walk the line" whenever they see one (painter's tape, curb, sidewalk crack, etc.).

Balance and Vestibular

"Slow is good!"

♥ Fun ♥

- ♥ Have the children step over a small item placed on the "beam."
  Examples:
  - ♥ Mini pumpkin
  - ♥ Stuffed animal
- ♥ Have the children stop midway on the "beam" and do a Flamingo pose. You can place an "X" with painter's tape to show them where to stop and pose.
- ♥ Have the child reach the "X" and turn around and return to start point.

LEARNING Stage 1

- The child may be wobbly or unable to stay on the the full length of the "beam."
- The child may take wider steps while walking on the "beam."

WORKING Stage 2

- The child may be able to stay on most, but not the entire length, of the "beam."
- The child takes mainly heel-to-toe steps while walking on the "beam."

GOT IT! Stage 3

- The children are able to walk heel-to-toe entire length of the "beam."

☺ **Start where the child is at.** For example, if a child is at Stage 2, begin there and progress forward. For more information see page 22.

Balance and Vestibular

Hopscotch

To develop balance skills.

TEACHER TOOLBOX
- Hopscotch mat

Note:
☐ Hopscotch is a lead up skill to skipping.

How to do it

This activity is written as individual use for safety.
It is intended to be used in a S.M.A.R.T. course where all children participate.

1. Teacher model, if possible, or use a child to model.

2. Have the child begin at the bottom and jump with both feet on each spot in order.

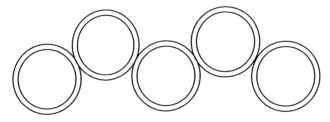

3. When the child is able to complete the mat, in control and staying inside the lines, she may move to the next step in the progression listed below.

Next steps of progression:
  (1) Hop with the right foot only
  (2) Hop with the left foot only
  (3) Alternate hopping with one foot and then jumping with two feet

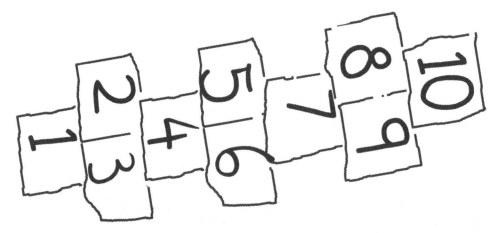

Balance and Vestibular

That's one S.M.A.R.T. Teacher!

- **Elissa in Detroit Lakes** makes her Hopscotch mat out of clip art. She enlarges the image to a full sheet of paper, makes multiple copies, laminates and adheres them to the floor. During an animals theme she made huge bear paws.

- **Edie in Park Rapids** tapes hoops together in springtime and she tells the children they are jumping in "puddles."

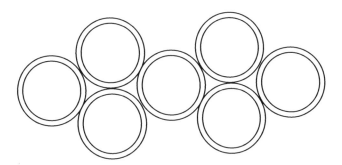

LEARNING Stage 1
- The child may be able to jump with both feet on each square in numerical order.
- The child may not make the full length of the mat.

WORKING Stage 2
- The child can jump with both feet on each square in numerical order the full length of the mat.
- The child can alternate hopping with one foot and then jumping with two feet, but may not make the full length of the mat.

GOT IT! Stage 3
- The children can alternate hopping with one foot and then jumping with two feet the full length of the mat.

☺ **Start where the child is at.** For example, if a child is at Stage 2, begin there and progress forward. For more information see page 22.

Balance and Vestibular

© 2011, A Chance To Grow, Inc. S.M.A.R.T. Pre-K CORE Program Guide • 43

Rebounder

TEACHER TOOLBOX
- Rebounder

To develop gross motor, balance and whole body learning.

How to do it

This activity is written as individual use for safety. **It is intended to be used in a S.M.A.R.T. Course where all children participate.**

1. Teacher model, if possible, or use a child to model.
2. Have the child jump up and down on the Rebounder using both feet.
3. Have the child count to 10.

♥ Fun ♥

- ♥ Have the child wave a scarf or bandana while jumping.
- ♥ Have the child jump while saying items on Learning Ladders*.

🛑 SAFETY FIRST

- Teach the children to step onto the Rebounder safely.
- Teach them to step down from the Rebounder safely.
- Make sure there are no obstructions on Rebounder.

***LEARNING LADDERS ACTIVITY** can be found in **Get to the MORE of Readiness,** the CORE companion book. Available from www.actg.com/smartprek

That's one S.M.A.R.T. Teacher!

 Donna in Coon Rapids does jumping activities with her whole class at the end of her S.M.A.R.T. Course time. The children line up on the mat and jump to her directions. *"Jump in place 8 times." "Jump with both hands up 5 times."*

 Kristi in Anoka has her children practice counting on while jumping on the Rebounder. In the middle of the year she has them count from 10 and count to 20. Later she has count from 15 to 30.

Balance and Vestibular

Gross Motor Activities

Developmentally, Gross Motor leads to Fine Motor. We start with big movements that provide a foundation for our bodies to understand smaller, more refined movements.

1. Alligator Crawl
2. Slap Track
3. Free Creep
4. Overhead Ladder
5. Cross Patterning

Notes on Gross Motor:

_____
_____
_____
_____
_____
_____
_____
_____
_____
_____
_____
_____
_____
_____

Read more about Gross Motor:

- www.ot-mom-learning-activities.com/preschool-gross-motor-activities.html
- www.preschools4all.com/gross-motor-activities-for-preschoolers.html
- familyfitness.about.com/od/preschoolers/a/grossmotorskill.htm
- www.sensory-processing-disorder.com/index.html
- www.brighthub.com/education/early-childhood/articles/44170.aspx

Catalogs

- www.sportime.com
- www.gophersport.com

Gross Motor

Alligator Crawl

TEACHER TOOLBOX
- Linoleum floor space of 15 - 18 feet

OR
- (2) 4 x 8 mats = 16 feet

OR
- Vinyl carpet runner of 15 - 18 feet

To develop coordination at the basic level and integrate both sides of the brain.

How to do it

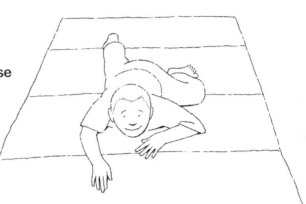

This activity is written as individual use for safety.
It is intended to be used in a S.M.A.R.T. Course where all children participate.

1. Teacher model, if possible, or use a child to model.

2. Begin Alligator Crawling on a linoleum floor, mat or vinyl carpet runner.

3. Have the child Alligator Crawl on her stomach using the opposite arm and leg simultaneously (a cross pattern). For example, the child would move the left arm and right leg and then the right arm and left leg.

4. You should observe the following as the child Alligator Crawls with her entire body flat on the mat:
   - The arm extends as it reaches, as in swimming
   - The side of each foot digs in and pushes off
   - The leg flexes in a 90-degree angle
   - The hands are flat and pull as they come toward the shoulders
   - The hand flips slightly before the arm extends again (supination)
   - The chin is approximately one inch off the floor or mat
   - The chest remains flat on the floor or mat throughout the activity

5. You may use occasional reminders such as, *"keep your hands flat"* or *"dig your toes,"* but keep in mind <u>the children should do this automatically rather than thinking about it.</u>

 The Alligator Crawl **DOES NOT** include scooter boards.

Gross Motor

© 2011, A Chance To Grow, Inc.

That's one S.M.A.R.T. Teacher!

- **Cassie in Coon Rapids** demonstrates the Alligator Crawl to her children! She gets down on the floor and shows them exactly how it is done.
- **Mary in Forest Lake** has her children transition to the S.M.A.R.T. Room doing the Alligator Crawl! They all crawl down the hall.

LEARNING Stage 1

- Initially the child may Alligator Crawl using the left arm and left leg and then the right arm and right leg. This is called a homolateral crawl. A child with a homolateral crawl should be allowed to continue crawling in this fashion, **but it is not to be taught.** It is important to recognize, with enough crawling, the homolateral pattern will mature into a cross pattern (left arm and right leg and then right arm and left leg). A child with a homolateral crawl can benefit from EXTRA Alligator Crawling.

♥ Fun Stuff ♥

- ♥ Alligator Crawling may be done under and around desks and large chairs.
- ♥ See S.M.A.R.T. Courses (on page 93) for more Fun Ideas!

WORKING Stage 2

- The child may be able to crawl with a cross pattern and may reach straight out from the shoulders. Again, **it is not to be taught**, but it may occur. Have the child Alligator Crawl on a line. The midline of her body is placed on the line. When her hand comes up she places her hand on the line.
- The child may not be able to push off with the side of the foot.

GOT IT! Stage 3

- The children are able to crawl on any surface with a cross pattern, or using the opposite arm and leg simultaneously. They also have supination, or a slight flip of the hand before the arm extends again while crawling forward. You will note the ease by which the children crawl and a pattern of two beats as the opposite hand and leg land on the mat, first one set then the other for two beats.

☺ **Start where the child is at.** For example, if a child is at Stage 2, begin there and progress forward. For more information see page 22.

 Gross Motor

Alligator Crawl in a S.M.A.R.T. Course

⚠️ When using the Alligator Crawl in an S.M.A.R.T. Course, be sure to leave space in between the children for safety, at least 8 feet. Use a taped line to help the children self-monitor. *"When the child in front of you gets to the tape line it is safe for you to go."*

Things to Alligator Crawl on:

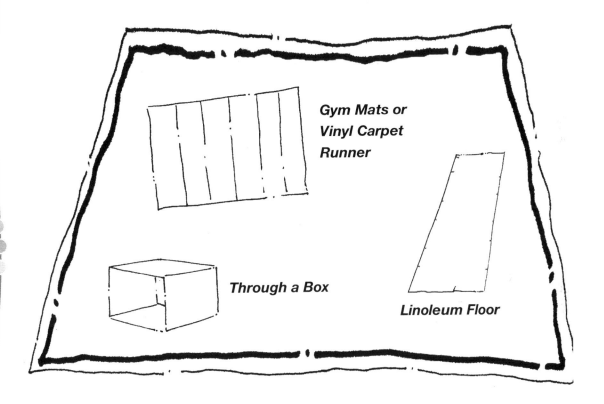

Gym Mats or Vinyl Carpet Runner

Through a Box

Linoleum Floor

That's one S.M.A.R.T. Teacher!

- 🍎 **Edie in Park Rapids** uses a pet toy containing a squeaker with the Alligator Crawl. When her children get to the toy they give it a squeak! Of course, she places the toy at the very END to encourage her children to crawl the full length of the mat.

- 🍎 **Deb in Detroit Lakes** has been known to wear fun slippers during S.M.A.R.T. time. Her children chase after them while crawling on the floor or down a mat.

- 🍎 **Beth in Columbia Heights** aims her laser point on the mat just beyond a child's hand. The child reaches out with each hand and chases the red dot down the mat.

Gross Motor

© 2011, A Chance To Grow, Inc. S.M.A.R.T. Pre-K CORE Program Guide • 49

Slap Track

To develop balance, depth perception, eye-hand coordination, bilateral coordination and eye teaming.

TEACHER TOOLBOX
- Clear 12 gauge vinyl, 10 feet long

OR
- Clear plastic shower Curtain, 5 feet tall

AND
- 5 1/2" x 8 1/2" strips of plastic for pockets. Clear page protectors work well
- Good quality clear packing tape
- 5" x 8" white unlined index cards

How to do it

This activity is written as individual use for safety.
It is intended to be used in a S.M.A.R.T. Course where all children participate.

1. Teacher model, if possible, or use a child to model.
2. You should observe the following as the child creeps down the Slap Track:
   - The hands are flat and gently slap each card
   - The fingers are slightly separated and pointing forward
   - The back remains flat throughout the activity
   - The eyes turn from side to side as the child looks at each card
   - The feet are relaxed with toes dragging on the track
   - The movement is fluid, without stopping to "decode" the material
   - The child creeps slowly

"Slow is good!"

3. Have the children say the name of the color or picture on the card as the hand strikes it. The object is to have both eyes looking at the card just before the hand hits the floor.

4. You may use occasional reminders such as, **"keep your hands flat"** or **"slap the cards,"** but keep in mind <u>the children should do this automatically rather than thinking about it.</u>

 Have the child look at each pocket just before the hand strikes the floor.

When using the Slap Track in an obstacle course, be sure to leave space in between the children for safety at least 5 feet.

 Gross Motor

That's one S.M.A.R.T. Teacher!

Edie in Park Rapids occasionally fills her Slap Track pockets with a variety of textures. She puts some items in zipper top bags: hair gel, play dough, etc. Other items she puts into the pockets: cotton balls, bubble wrap, a noise maker from inside a toy, etc.

Slip product in pocket on back side of Slap Track

LEARNING Stage 1

Make sure the first pocket is on the <u>right side</u> when <u>using</u> the Slap Track.

- Initially the child may creep using the left hand and left knee and then the right hand and right knee. This is called a homolateral creep. A child with a homolateral creep should be allowed to continue creeping in this fashion, **but it is not to be taught.** It is important to recognize, with enough creeping, the homolateral pattern will mature into a cross pattern (left hand and right knee and then right hand and left knee). A child with a homolateral creep can benefit from EXTRA creeping.

WORKING Stage 2

- The child may be able to creep with a cross pattern but may turn the hands inward or outward and/or lift her toes up off of the floor. Again, **it is not to be taught**, but it may occur.

GOT IT! Stage 3

- The children are able to creep on hands and knees using the opposite arm and leg simultaneously. For example, they would move the left hand and right knee and then the right hand and left knee. The children should move at a slow and even pace. ***"Slow is good!"***

☺ ***Start where the child is at.*** For example, if a child is at Stage 2, begin there and progress forward. For more information see page 22.

Gross Motor

How to Make Two Slap Tracks

1. Purchase clear vinyl from a fabric or home improvement store or a clear plastic shower curtain from a discount store.

Clear Vinyl	Shower Curtain
a. Cut a width of the vinyl to be 18˝ x 10´. b. Repeat with remaining section of vinyl. You will have 3 vinyl lengths of 18˝ x 10´.	a. Cut the shower curtain into four equal widths of 18˝ x 5´. b. Tape 2 of these widths together lengthwise to make an 18˝ x 10´ Slap Track. Repeat with remaining lengths.

2. Cut 5 1/2˝ X 8 1/2˝ plastic pockets, you will need approximately 13 for each 10´ Slap Track (26 pockets total).

3. Spacing for Slap Track pockets is: 9˝ for 3 - 5 year olds.

4. Using this distance as a guide, place a plastic pocket onto the LEFT bottom corner of the plastic runner and apply with packing tape on the top, bottom and INNER sides to form a pocket. The outside edge should be open, so that a card may be easily slid into the pocket.

5. Next, from the bottom, measure 9˝ up the right side. Place the bottom of the next plastic pocket at that 9˝ mark. Tape this pocket as described above.

6. Now, place the next pocket on the left side 9" up from the last pocket and continue to alternate the pockets from left to right up the length of the runner. The pockets should appear to be evenly spaced the full length of the Slap Track.

7. Flip the runner over and insert 5˝ x 8˝ cards into the pockets of the Slap Track. See Slap Track Pocket Ideas on the next page.

Note:

☐ When <u>making</u> the Slap Track you will tape the first pocket onto the LEFT side. When you use it, you will flip it over so the first pocket is on the RIGHT side.

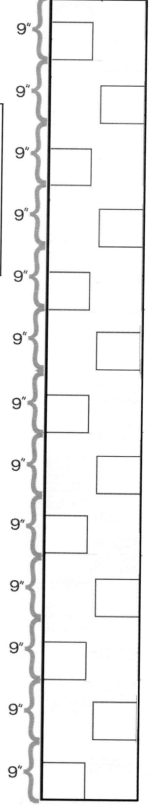

This is a diagram of the back side assembly of your Slap Track.

Gross Motor

Slap Track Pocket Ideas

1. Start with "HIGH FIVE" and fill pockets with hand art (simply copy masters on next page, cut and place into pockets), starting with one color.

2. Progress to 2 colors.
   For example: red - blue - red - blue - red - blue

3. Next progress to repeating patterns of 2 colors.
   For example: red - red - blue - red - red - blue

4. Continue with shapes, theme items or letters in the same color (avoid mixing too many items).
   For example: circle - square - circle - square

Note:
- ☐ **K.I.S.S.**
  Keeping it simple is S.M.A.R.T.
- ☐ The information should be MASTERED material, not instructional material (this allows for fluid movement through the track).

 Start with 2 variations, go to 3, but never more than 4. Repeat the sequence.

 Avoid the TEACHER TRAP

If the child has to stop and think, you have made it too difficult by:
- Using too much information too fast—too many colors, shapes, letters or numbers
- Using random patterns or mixing too many items together

Many **SLAP TRACK POCKET MASTERS** are available in our companion book, **S.M.A.R.T. Pre-K Themes & Masters CORE Fun!**

Available from
www.actg.org/smartprek

Gross Motor

© 2011, A Chance To Grow, Inc.

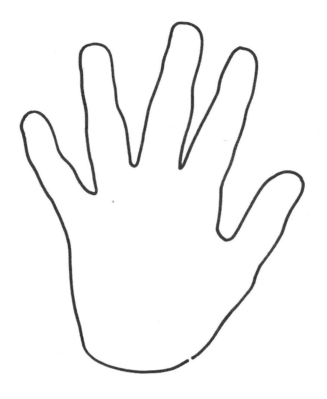

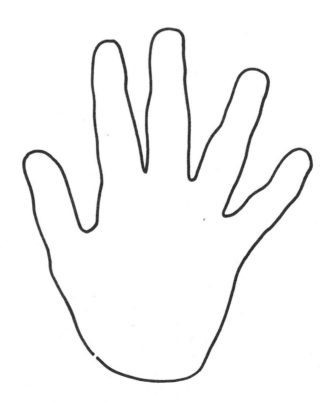

Free Creep

To develop balance, depth perception, eye-hand coordination, bilateral coordination and eye teaming.

TEACHER TOOLBOX
- Open floor space

♥ Fun Stuff ♥

♥ Use as a transition back to table or circle time.

♥ **Doggie, Doggie, where's your bone?** Scatter small objects or "bones" on the floor and have the child creep to find her bone!

♥ **Circus Ponies** Turn on the music and have children creep until the music stops.

♥ Use a fabric tunnel or make one with boxes. Be sure to secure it to the floor.

How to do it

This activity is written as individual use for safety. **It is intended to be used in a S.M.A.R.T. Course where all children participate.**

1. Teacher model, if possible, or use a child to model.

2. Have the child creep on hands and knees using the opposite arm and leg simultaneously. For example, the child would move the left hand and right knee and then the right hand and left knee. The child should move at a slow and even pace. *"Slow is good!"*

3. You should observe the following as the child creeps:
   - The hands are flat and gently slap the ground
   - The fingers are slightly separated and pointing forward
   - The back remains flat throughout the activity
   - The eyes turn from side to side as the child looks at each hand
   - The feet are relaxed with toes dragging on the ground
   - The movement is fluid
   - The child creeps slowly

4. You may use occasional reminders such as, *"keep your hands flat"* or *"slap the ground,"* but keep in mind <u>the children should do this automatically rather than thinking about it.</u>

"Slow is good!"

⚠ Do not replace Slap Track with Free Creep. Use for additional practice.

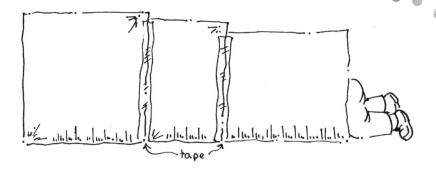

LEARNING Stage 1

- Initially the child may creep using the left hand and left knee and then the right hand and right knee. This is called a homolateral creep. A child with a homolateral creep should be allowed to continue creeping in this fashion, **but it is not to be taught.** It is important to recognize, with enough creeping, the homolateral pattern will mature into a cross pattern (left hand and right knee and then right hand and left knee). A child with a homolateral creep can benefit from EXTRA creeping.

That's one S.M.A.R.T. Teacher!

🍎 **Deb in Detroit Lakes** uses a red tunnel. The week her children visit the Apple Orchard, they practice being worms in the big, red apple.

WORKING Stage 2

- The child may be able to creep with a cross pattern but may turn the hands inward or outward and/or lift her toes up off of the floor. Again, **it is not to be taught**, but it may occur.

GOT IT! Stage 3

- The children are able to creep on hands and knees using the opposite arm and leg simultaneously. For example, they would move the left hand and right knee and then the right hand and left knee. The children should move at a slow and even pace.
"Slow is good!"

☺ **Start where the child is at.** For example, if a child is at Stage 2, begin there and progress forward. For more information see page 22.

 Gross Motor

Overhead Ladder

To develop upper body strength, eye-hand coordination, eye teaming and to increase oxygen intake.

TEACHER TOOLBOX
- Adjustable Overhead Ladder
- Gym mats

Note:
☐ Blueprints for the Adjustable Overhead Ladder can be found at: www.actg.org/smartprek

How to do it

This activity is written as individual use for safety. **It is intended to be used in a S.M.A.R.T. Course where all children participate.**

1. Teacher model, if possible, or use a child to model.

   ⚠ In the beginning, the child can hang for up to a count of 10 to build up strength before working on moving from rung to rung.

   Hang with one arm and then the other arm separately to build strength in each arm.

2. Have the child move from rung to rung while visually tracking each hand as it moves forward. The child should wrap her thumbs around the rung, like a motorcycle.

"This is a motorcycle grip"

Remember to adjust the height of the ladder to the child's height with her arms extended over her head, plus 6 inches.

Gross Motor

SAFETY FIRST

- It is important to teach the children how to drop safely. They should practice by holding onto the rung, preparing for a drop with bent knees and hands to their side.

- The Adjustable Overhead Ladder should be adjusted to the child's height with her arms extended over her head, plus 6 inches. **Use an average height with groups of children.**

- Adjust the height of the ladder so the drop is no more than 6 inches.

- Also, ensure the children use a "motorcycle grip" for safety, as well as for fine motor development.

- Gym mats should be placed under the Overhead Ladder.

- Do not allow the child to do this activity if she has blisters on her hands.

- Wrap rungs with tennis racket grip tape for extra traction and cushion.

LEARNING Stage 1

- The child cannot move from rung to rung. Allow her to hang from the first rung for up to a count of 10. Adjust the time to what the child is capable of doing.

WORKING Stage 2

- The child is able to complete a few rungs. You can occasionally help her begin near the end of the rungs and complete the Overhead Ladder. This allows her a sense of completing the activity.

GOT IT! Stage 3

- The children can move from rung to rung, without assistance, completing the full length of the Overhead Ladder.

☺ **Start where the child is at.** For example, if a child is at Stage 2, begin there and progress forward. For more information see page 22.

 Gross Motor

Cross Patterning

To develop cross pattern movement and integrate both sides of the brain.

How to do it

1. Teacher model, if possible, or use a child to model.
2. Place a sticker on the top of the children's right hands and left knees.
3. Have the children slap the hand with the sticker onto the knee with the sticker while they are sitting on the floor.
4. Have the children slap the hand without the sticker onto the knee without the sticker.
5. Repeat.
6. When the children are able to Cross Pattern successfully while sitting, they may move to the next step in the progression listed below.

Next steps of progression:

(1) Cross Pattern while standing
(2) Cross Pattern while walking

♥ Fun Stuff ♥

- **Criss Cross Apple Sauce** Recite Criss Cross Apple Sauce (touch each knee with opposite hand). Spiders crawling up your back (hands wiggle upward). Cool breeze (hands wave and cross above head). Tight squeeze (hands hug self). Now you get the shivers (shake off). Repeat.
- When the children know how to Cross Pattern while walking you can turn on some march music and have them Cross Pattern march around the room.

TEACHER TOOLBOX
- Colored stickers

Note:

- ☐ As children gain skills discontinue the use of the stickers.
- ☐ Use Cross Patterning while walking during transitions to the classroom, playground, to circle time or with music.
- ☐ This activity may be integrated into a S.M.A.R.T. Course between two areas or if a child is waiting at any time she can Cross Pattern in place.

Gross Motor

© 2011, A Chance To Grow, Inc.

That's one S.M.A.R.T. Teacher!

- **Donna in Coon Rapids** uses two colors of small plastic plates with this activity. She gives each child one plate of each color. The group sits on the carpet in a circle and she leads, starting with both plates in the air. ***"Cross the yellow and touch the opposite knee"*** and the children tap the opposite knee with the plate. ***"Now, cross the purple and touch the other knee."*** She repeats this several times on each side.

- **Leslie in Drexel** has a spot the children pass everyday to practice cross pattern walking. After two weeks, her children automatically start cross pattern walking from the "Criss Cross Tree" to the classroom door.

- **Jodee in Brooklyn Park** places a picture of a treasure chest with an "X Marks The Spot" on which her little pirates Cross Pattern.

LEARNING
Stage 1

- Initially, the child cannot cross over the middle of her body. She may use the right hand/right knee and then the left hand/left knee. This called a homolateral pattern. You can assist her by sitting behind and moving her arms to cross the middle of her body.

WORKING
Stage 2

- The child may be able to cross over the middle of her body some of the time or may have segmented movements during the activity. With enough exposure this will mature.

GOT IT!
Stage 3

- The children are able to cross over the middle of their bodies using opposite hand and knee simultaneously. For example, they would use the right hand and left knee and then the left hand and right knee. The children should move at a slow and even pace. ***"Slow is good!"***

☺ **Start where the child is at.** For example, if a child is at Stage 2, begin there and progress forward. For more information see page 22.

Gross Motor

60 • S.M.A.R.T. Pre-K CORE Program Guide © 2011, A Chance To Grow, Inc.

CORE Vision Activities

Sight and vision are NOT the same.
We believe 20/20 is not enough.

Vision is a complex process involving over 20 visual abilities and more than 65% of all of the pathways to the brain.

Eye Movements

1. Tactile Trackers
2. Flower Power
3. Swinging Ball
4. Driver's Ed
5. Magic Erasers
6. Thumbs Up
7. Loop de Loos
8. Overs and Unders

Focusing

1. Basic Vision
2. Near / Far Focus

Notes on CORE Vision:

Most of these activities work in more than one area of vision.

> ⚠ In this section we work on **Visual Efficiency Skills, which help children see:** clearly, singly, comfortably with both eyes AND at a variety of distances.

Note: ✎

☐ Normal visual acuity (clear vision) is necessary for performance of the above techniques. Therefore all children should be evaluated for visual acuity via professional eye examination or Snellen Chart screening. Children should wear their prescribed corrective lenses during the activities (unless the glasses are specifically designed for near work only or for distance only).

Read more about Vision:

- www.oepf.org
- www.covd.org
- www.eyecanlearn.com
- www.visionandlearning.org
- pavevision.org

CORE Vision

Eye Movement Activities

Eye Movement Control is the ability to move the eyes together quickly, accurately and in precise coordination. Accurate eye movements are needed in order to accurately perform many tasks such as:

- *reading along lines of text*
- *scanning vertical columns*
- *making accurate shifts from desk to board*
- *tracking in sport activities*

Eye Movements

1. Tactile Trackers
2. Flower Power
3. Swinging Ball
4. Driver's Ed
5. Magic Erasers
6. Thumbs Up
7. Loop de Loos
8. Overs and Unders

Tactile Trackers

To develop smooth pursuit eye movements and eye-hand coordination skills.

TEACHER TOOLBOX
- Poster board
- Markers
- Glue
- Magnets or Velcro (or something to hang the Tactile Tracker on the wall)
- A variety of yarn, pipe cleaners, thin dowels, metal rings, puffy paint, etc.

How to do it

This activity is written as individual use, <u>but can be done in small groups of 2 - 3 children.</u>

1. Teacher model, if possible, or use a child to model.

2. Have the child stand in front of the Tactile Tracker with the center of the circle at the height of their nose.

3. Have the child cover their left eye with their left hand and extend their right hand to the Tactile Tracker with the elbow slightly bent.

4. Using their right pointer finger, have the child start at the dot and trace on the line following your directions. Go very slowly in each direction two times.

5. Have the child cover the right eye with the right hand and use their left pointer finger. Repeat your directions.

6. Repeat and have the child use both eyes together and the dominant hand.

The entire sequence must be done for this activity.

 "Slow is good!"
The child's eye movements should be smooth and fluid <u>without any movement of the head.</u>
This activity is be done on a vertical surface. Horizontal surfaces are much more visually challenging.

CORE Vision - Eye Movements

How to make Tactile Trackers

1. Draw a 10" circle or trace a 10" plate onto the poster board in one color with a marker. Include a dot as a starting point.

2. Use the glue to "trace" a line, allowing a thin track of glue on top of the circle.

3. Allow to dry.

4. Hang the Tactile Tracker circle up on the wall using magnets or Velcro so that the height is adjustable.

♥ Fun Stuff ♥

- ♥ Make sure to use a variety of tactile items when making additional Tactile Trackers.
- ♥ New patterns can be made following the same procedures, and include:
  - ♥ Shapes ♥ Letters ♥ Numbers ♥ Simple Mazes

That's one S.M.A.R.T. Teacher!

- **Cindy in Stillwater** hangs her Tactile Trackers just outside the restrooms. She sends in one half of her group while the other half does the Tactile Trackers and vice versa.

- **Beth in Columbia Heights** makes one Tactile Tracker for each letter of the alphabet, A to Z. Her children love the variety and never get bored! She uses a WIDE variety of tactile items including: zippers, feathers, foil, dots and just about anything she finds in her arts and crafts supplies.

LEARNING Stage 1

- Initially, the child may not trace on the line and her eye movements may be jerky. Continued repetitions over time will increase accuracy.

WORKING Stage 2

- The child may not trace on the line at times and her eye movements may be slightly jerky. Repetitions, over time, will result in smooth eye movements.

GOT IT! Stage 3

- The children are able to trace on the line for the entire duration of the activity and their eye movements are smooth.

☺ **Start where the child is at.** For example, if a child is at Stage 2, begin there and progress forward. For more information see page 22.

CORE Vision - Eye Movements

Flower Power

To develop smooth pursuit eye movements and eye-hand coordination skills.

TEACHER TOOLBOX
- Commercially made flower

OR
- Handmade flower with eyes

How to do it

This activity is written as individual use, but can be done in small groups of 2 - 3 children.

 The entire sequence must be done for this activity.

1. Teacher model, if possible, or use a child to model.

2. Have the child cover her left eye with her left hand.

3. You should face the child and move the flower slowly.
   - First move it in a circle
   - Then horizontally
   - Then vertically
   - Finally diagonally

4. Go very slowly in each direction two times. The child follows the target while keeping her head still.

5. Have the child cover the right eye with the right hand and repeat the direction above.

6. Have the child use both eyes together and repeat the direction above.

 "Slow is good!"
The child's eye movements should be smooth and fluid without any movement of the head.

CORE Vision - Eye Movements

That's one S.M.A.R.T. Teacher!

- **Elissa in Detroit Lakes** created this activity! Originally, it was suggested to use a pencil with a topper. Elissa substituted a large commercially made flower and her children loved it.

- **Sandy in Oakdale** does Flower Power during "choice time." She calls over her children one at a time and follows the sequence with each child individually. This REALLY increases the quality and benefits of the activity.

- **Missy in Frazee** uses Flower Power as a dismissal activity when working with small groups. She follows the sequence with each child individually. This REALLY increases the quality and benefits of the activity. When the child is done, they can choose one of the following from the flower; a hug, a handshake or neither, then they transition to the next activity.

♥ Fun Stuff ♥

- When making your own Flower Power flower, we encourage you to use your creativity.
- Pool noodles are a fun way to make a large flower, or even a person! Glue large pom poms, google eyes and maybe even pipe cleaners for hair and a smile!

LEARNING Stage 1
- Initially, the child's eye movements may be jerky. Continued repetitions over time will increase accuracy.

WORKING Stage 2
- The child's eye movements may be slightly jerky. Repetitions, over time, will result in smooth eye movements.

GOT IT! Stage 3
- The children have smooth eye movements for the entire duration for the activity.

☺ **Start where the child is at.** For example, if a child is at Stage 2, begin there and progress forward. For more information see page 22.

CORE Vision - Eye Movements

Swinging Ball

To develop and enhance eye movement skills.

TEACHER TOOLBOX
- 4 - 6 inch sponge type or soft ball
- String

How to do it

This activity is written as individual use, but can be done in small groups of 2 - 3 children.

1. Teacher model, if possible, or use a child to model.

2. Have the child stand in front of the Swinging Ball. Adjust the ball so that it is suspended near the bridge of her nose.

3. The child should take a step back, so when she points at it with extended arms her fingertips just touch the ball.

4. The child moves the ball by tapping it gently. The ball should move slowly to try to control eye movements as precisely as possible.

♥ Fun Stuff ♥

♥ Have the child tap the ball with her elbows.

 "Slow is good!"
The child's eye movements should be smooth and fluid without any movement of the head. Check with the child to make sure she can follow the ball.

 CORE Vision - Eye Movements

How to make the Swinging Ball

1. Pierce the ball with a needle threaded with the string. Pull the needle and string through the ball and knot it on the other side of the ball.

2. Suspend the Swinging Ball from the ceiling. Use enough string to allow the ball to go to the floor with the end of the string hanging next to the ball.

3. The Swinging Ball should be able to move up and down freely. When storing, pull the string so the ball is near the ceiling and out of view.

That's one S.M.A.R.T. Teacher!

- **Monica in Coon Rapids** uses this activity right after calendar time. She lowers the ball down in front of the calendar and swings if for all her children to track at one time.

- **Leslie in Drexel** hangs her Swinging Ball in the hallway. She has all of her children do it with their backs against the wall and then swings the ball for all to follow with their eyes.

♥ Fun Stuff ♥

♥ Place small colored stickers on the ball and have the child say the color as she taps.

LEARNING Stage 1

- Initially, the child's eye movements may be jerky. It may be necessary for the child to lay down underneath the ball to increase the accuracy of the eye movements.

WORKING Stage 2

- The child's eye movements may be slightly jerky. Repetitions, over time, will result in smooth eye movements.

GOT IT! Stage 3

- The children have smooth eye movements for the entire duration for the activity.

☺ **Start where the child is at.** For example, if a child is at Stage 2, begin there and progress forward. For more information see page 22.

CORE Vision - Eye Movements

© 2011, A Chance To Grow, Inc.

Driver's Ed

To develop smooth pursuit eye movements and eye-hand coordination skills.

TEACHER TOOLBOX
- Poster board
- Markers
- Homemade "driver's licenses" (optional)
- Chalkboard or whiteboard (optional)
- Chalk or whiteboard markers (optional)
- Miniature toy car

How to do it

This activity is written as individual use, but can be done in small groups of 2 - 3 children.

1. Teacher model, if possible, or use a child to model.

2. Have the child drive the toy car within the boundaries. The child must keep the car in the "middle of the road." Go very slowly in each direction two times.

Note:
☐ This activity can be done on a chalk or whiteboard

3. When the child is successful, she may "drive" on the road that curves.

 "Slow is good!"

The child's eye movements should be smooth and fluid <u>without any movement of the head</u>.

Start this activity on a vertical surface. Horizontal surfaces are much more visually challenging

When the child is successful you can move to a horizontal surface.

CORE Vision - Eye Movements

How to make Driver's Ed

1. Use poster board and markers to design a road on which a toy car will drive.

2. Make two parallel lines 2 inches apart on one side of the poster board. On the other side of the poster board make a similar road that curves.

♥ Fun Stuff ♥

- ♥ Make a homemade "driver's license" for the child to receive when she successfully stays on the road.
- ♥ Make a series of roads, decreasing the space between the lines that make the road and increasing the curves or zigzags in the road.
- ♥ Draw the road on the full length of the chalkboard or whiteboard. Have the child "drive" her car on road.

That's one S.M.A.R.T. Teacher!

🍎 **Jodee in Brooklyn Park** uses emergency vehicles as children gain skills to increase speed. She also hangs a car or city carpet on the wall.

LEARNING Stage 1

- Initially, the child's eye movements may be jerky. Continued repetitions over time will increase accuracy.

WORKING Stage 2

- The child's eye movements may be slightly jerky. Repetitions, over time, will result in smooth eye movements.

GOT IT! Stage 3

- The children have smooth eye movements for the entire duration for the activity.

☺ **Start where the child is at.** For example, if a child is at Stage 2, begin there and progress forward. For more information see page 22.

CORE Vision - Eye Movements

© 2011, A Chance To Grow, Inc. S.M.A.R.T. Pre-K CORE Program Guide • 71

Magic Erasers

To develop smooth pursuit eye movements and eye-hand coordination skills.

TEACHER TOOLBOX
- Small whiteboard
- Dry Erase marker(s) with felt tops

How to do it

This activity is written as individual use, but can be done in small groups of 2 - 3 children.

1. Teacher model, if possible, or use a child to model.

2. Have the child draw a line or shape on the white board using the Dry Erase marker.

3. Have the child erase the line she created by using the felt top on the marker. Tell the child *"The top is magic, see how it erases the line when you trace right on top of it?"*

That's one S.M.A.R.T. Teacher!

- **Priscilla in Oakdale** has her children erase using the "old" Dry Erase marker(s)! When the marker is dried out, she puts a piece of colored tape around the end and her children know which are the writing markers and which are the erasing markers.

 "Slow is good!"
The child's eye movements should be smooth and fluid <u>without any movement of the head</u>.

Start this activity on a vertical surface. Horizontal surfaces are much more visually challenging. When the child is successful you can move to a horizontal surface.

 CORE Vision - Eye Movements

That's one S.M.A.R.T. Teacher!

🍎 **Deb in Detroit Lakes** glues small pom poms on the tops of markers. Her children use the colorful pom poms to erase the line.

♥ Fun Stuff ♥

- ♥ Make apple trees and tell the children *"pick the apples"* by erasing them.
- ♥ Put a line of ants on the board and have the children get rid of them *"One by One - Hurrah!"*
- ♥ You can make items for the children to erase such as:
  - ♥ Shapes
  - ♥ Letters
  - ♥ Number
  - ♥ Name

LEARNING — **Stage 1**
- Initially, the child's eye movements may be jerky. Continued repetitions over time will increase accuracy.

WORKING — **Stage 2**
- The child's eye movements may be slightly jerky. Repetitions, over time, will result in smooth eye movements.

GOT IT! — **Stage 3**
- The children have smooth eye movements for the entire duration for the activity.

☺ ***Start where the child is at.*** For example, if a child is at Stage 2, begin there and progress forward. For more information see page 22.

CORE Vision - Eye Movements

Thumbs Up

To develop saccadic eye movements and eye-hand coordination skills.

TEACHER TOOLBOX
- Paper towel tube
- (2) different colors of tape
- (2) different small stickers

How to do it

This activity is written as individual use, but can be done in small groups of 2 - 3 children.

1. Teacher model, if possible, or use a child to model.

2. Have the child hold the Thumbs Up tube with both hands, her thumbs facing her and just inside the stickers.

3. Have the child extend both arms at a natural reading length, about 12″ from their face. The child's shoulders and elbows should be in line.

4. Have the child look at one sticker or color and then look at the other sticker or color.

5. Have the child repeat looking from one sticker to the other a minimum of 6 times (8 - 10 times is optimal).

⚠ *"Slow is good!"*
The child's eye movements should be smooth and fluid without any movement of the head.

Start this activity on a vertical surface. Horizontal surfaces are much more visually challenging. When the child is successful you can move to a horizontal surface.

CORE Vision - Eye Movements

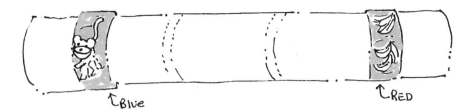
↳ Blue   ↳ Red

How to make Thumbs Up Tube

1. Using one color of tape, wrap around approximately 1 1/2" - 2" from the end the tube.
2. Repeat with the other color of tape on the other end of the tube.
3. Put one sticker on top of a piece of tape and the other sticker on top of the other piece of tape.

That's one S.M.A.R.T. Teacher!

 Priscilla in Oakdale uses the children's large name tags for this activity! She tells them to *"Look at the first letter in your name. Look at the last letter in your name."*

♥ Fun Stuff ♥

- ♥ Use different types of items for the children to look at such as:
  - ♥ Shapes   ♥ Letters   ♥ Numbers
- ♥ Substitute a paint stirring stick or a ruler for a more durable Thumbs Up stick.

LEARNING Stage 1
- Initially, the child's eye movements may be jerky, she may over and/or undershoot the "target." Continued repetitions over time will increase accuracy.

WORKING Stage 2

- The child's eye movements may be slightly jerky, she may occasionally over and/or undershoot the "target." Repetitions, over time, will result in smooth eye movements.

GOT IT! Stage 3

- The children have smooth eye movements for the entire duration for the activity.

☺ **Start where the child is at.** For example, if a child is at Stage 2, begin there and progress forward. For more information see page 22.

CORE Vision - Eye Movements

Loop de Loos

To develop saccadic eye movements and eye-hand coordination skills.

TEACHER TOOLBOX
- Chalkboard or whiteboard
- Piece of large chalk or Dry Erase marker

OR
- Loop de Loos sheet
- Pencil or crayon

Setting up the Loop de Loos

1. Draw a series of pictures on the board in a straight line or use a Loop de Loos sheet.

How to do it

This activity is written as individual use, <u>but can be done in small groups of 2 - 3 children.</u>

1. Teacher model, if possible, or use a child to model.

2. Have the child draw a continuous line under each row, looping each picture you indicate.

Example, *"Loop the circles."*

Example, *"Loop the squares."*

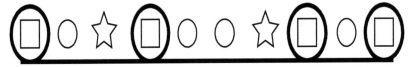

That's one S.M.A.R.T. Teacher!

 Priscilla in Oakdale uses plastic page protectors to save a tree! She slides her Loop de Loos sheet inside and has the children trace on the plastic with a Dry Erase marker.

 Leslie in Drexel uses numbers or letters for additional practice!

⚠️ *"Slow is good!"*

The child's eye movements should be smooth and fluid <u>without any movement of the head</u>.

Start this activity on a vertical surface. Horizontal surfaces are much more visually challenging. When the child is successful you can move to a horizontal surface.

CORE Vision - Eye Movements

Loop de Loos Sheet

LEARNING Stage 1

- Initially, the child's eye movements may be jerky, she may over and/or undershoot the "target." Continued repetitions over time will increase accuracy.

WORKING Stage 2

- The child's eye movements may be slightly jerky, she may occasionally over and/or undershoot the "target." Repetitions, over time, will result in smooth eye movements.

GOT IT! Stage 3

- The children have smooth eye movements for the entire duration for the activity.

☺ **Start where the child is at.** For example, if a child is at Stage 2, begin there and progress forward. For more information see page 22.

CORE Vision - Eye Movements

Overs and Unders

To develop saccadic eye movements and eye-hand coordination skills.

TEACHER TOOLBOX
- Chalkboard or whiteboard
- Piece of large chalk or Dry Erase marker

OR
- Overs and Unders sheet
- Pencil or crayon

Setting up the Overs and Unders

1. Select 2 shapes. Example, circles and squares.

2. In a straight line, draw a series of shapes in random pattern on the board.

3. Draw a continuous line under all of the "squares" and over all of the "circles" for the child to trace.

How to do it

This activity is written as individual use, but can be done in small groups of 2 - 3 children.

1. Teacher model, if possible, or use a child to model.

2. Have the child draw a continuous line under each row, looping each picture you indicate.

♥ Fun Stuff ♥

♥ Make thematic Overs and Unders sheets.

♥ Have the child complete multiple lines of Overs and Unders. When she gets to the end of one line she picks up her pencil and begins the next line.

♥ When the child is ready for a challenge, you can make Overs and Unders sheets without the line to trace.

That's one S.M.A.R.T. Teacher!

 Priscilla in Oakdale uses plastic page protectors to save a tree! She slides her Overs and Unders sheet inside and has the children trace on the plastic with a Dry Erase marker.

 Leslie in Drexel adds in some fun variations! The same activity could be done to learn letters or numbers.

 "Slow is good!"
The child's eye movements should be smooth and fluid without any movement of the head.

Start this activity on a vertical surface. Horizontal surfaces are much more visually challenging. When the child is successful you can move to a horizontal surface.

CORE Vision - Eye Movements

Overs and Unders

LEARNING Stage 1

- Initially, the child's eye movements may be jerky, she may over and/or undershoot the "target." Continued repetitions over time will increase accuracy.

WORKING Stage 2

- The child's eye movements may be slightly jerky, she may occasionally over and/or undershoot the "target." Repetitions, over time, will result in smooth eye movements.

GOT IT! Stage 3

- The children have smooth eye movements for the entire duration for the activity.

☺ **Start where the child is at.** For example, if a child is at Stage 2, begin there and progress forward. For more information see page 22.

CORE Vision - Eye Movements

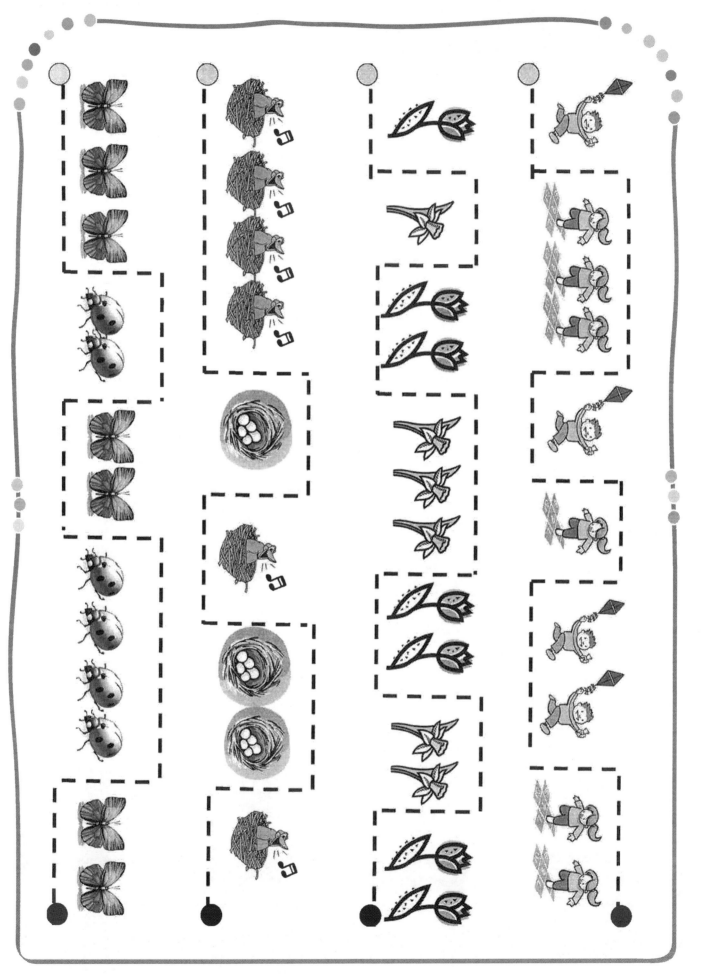

80 • S.M.A.R.T. Pre-K CORE Program Guide

© 2011, A Chance To Grow, Inc.

Focusing Activities

Focusing is the ability to see clearly and maintain that clarity:

- *at a fixed distance*
- *to shift focus from distance to near quickly, accurately and repeatedly*

Focusing

1. Basic Vision
2. Near / Far Focus

Basic Vision

To stimulate the most basic visual function (the pupillary reflex) and encourage focusing and visualization.

TEACHER TOOLBOX
- Dark room
- 75 - 100 watt light bulb
- Trouble light of corresponding wattage

How to do it

1. Teacher model, if possible, or use a child to model.

2. Have the children sit in a dark room, facing you.

3. Hold the trouble light towards the children and click the light on for 1 second.
   The children look directly toward the light.

4. Click the light off for approximately 5 seconds. A slow count to 5 works well.

5. Repeat for a total of 25 consecutive clicks, 1 second on and 5 seconds off.

That's one S.M.A.R.T. Teacher!

- **Edie in Park Rapids** reviews her entire curriculum every day during Basic Vision! She has cards with shapes, letters, numbers, names and vocabulary she shows when the light is on. Her students wait to say what they saw until the light is out. Edie ALSO created a Basic Vision room out of a small office! She has all of her students come into the room and sit down on two taped lines. It helps her students stay in place.

- **Kristi in Anoka** starts each year doing Basic Vision with some light in the room. Since some Pre-K children are afraid of the dark, she does this for the first two weeks of school until her students understand the activity.

⚠ When doing Basic Vision, it is better to error on the side of having the light on and/or off a little too long versus too short. The 5 (plus) seconds helps the eye "recover" before the light goes on again.

When using this as a group activity the children should change position in the room every day so that a child is not always sitting in the back or the front.

CORE Vision - Focusing

More S.M.A.R.T. Teachers!

- **Deb in Detroit Lakes** uses Basic Vision to teach her children to read their names! She writes all student names on large cards. When she shows "your name," then "you" are dismissed to wash your hands before lunch. She shuffles the cards everyday, so dismissal and exposure to the names is different. Deb reports that all children in her class, even the three year olds, know **ALL** the names by December!

- **Jocelyn in Coon Rapids** uses Basic Vision to review vocabulary! She has a small box of objects and pulls one object out to show when the light is on. Her children wait until the light is off to say what they saw, at which time she takes a new item out of the box. She changes the items every one to two weeks.

- **Cindy in Stillwater** has a Basic Vision binder. She has tabs for shapes, colors, letters and numbers. In each section she keeps the corresponding items in her curriculum. When it's time for Basic Vision, she is set to go!

♥ Fun Stuff ♥

- Have the children make faces that represent emotions. ***"Show me your happy face. Show me your surprised face. Show me your mad face."*** (Ask them when the light is off and they make the face when the light is on, one type of face for each click.)

- Have children clap out syllables to different words.

♥ More Fun ♥

- Have the children complete a phrase.

  Examples:
  mother and f____,
  salt and p____,
  aunt and un____.

- Have the children close off sentences.

  Example:
  The cat chased the m____.

♥ More Fun ♥

- Have the children state the opposite word in a sentence.

  Examples:
  The chair is black. (white)
  The coat was old. (new)
  My cat is big. (small)
  His rope is short. (long)

CORE Vision - Focusing

Adding in Academics:

Add in some fun variations! The same activity could be done using any of the following:

- **Same or Different:**

    Say 2 words.

    The children give a "thumbs up" for same OR "thumbs down" for different when the light is on.

    Examples: dug-bug, red-red, mush-much

- **Rhyme Time:**

    Say a phrase that ends with a word that can be rhymed.

    The children supply the correct word.

    Examples: A vehicle that rhymes with star. (car)

    A place that rhymes with spark. (park)

    A number that rhymes with door. (four)

- **Stretch a Word:** Have the children blend compound words.

    Examples: lady...bug

    rain...coat

    dog...house

- **Starts the Same:**

    Give the children a group of three words, starting with the same sound.

    Have the child say the beginning sound of all three.

    Examples: vase, vote, very /v/

    jump, jar, Jill /j/

SAME OR DIFFERENT, RHYME TIME, STRETCH A WORD AND STARTS THE SAME ACTIVITIES can be found in *Get to the MORE of Readiness,* the CORE companion book.

Available from www.actg.org/smartprek

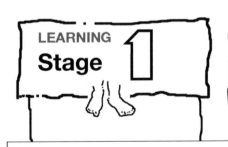

This activity is so basic there are no stages.

CORE Vision - Focusing

Near/Far Focus

To develop the ability to change focus from near to far and far to near.

TEACHER TOOLBOX
- Pencil with pencil topper
- Classroom objects

 The entire sequence must be done for this activity.

How to do it

This activity is written as individual use, but can be done in small groups of 2 - 3 children.

1. Teacher model, if possible, or use a child to model.

2. Have the child cover the right eye with right hand and hold the pencil with the left hand. The pencil should be directly in front of her nose at a distance of 4˝ - 6˝ and clearly in focus.

3. Have the child look quickly (about 2 seconds) to a picture, clock, or chair across the room, and then quickly (about 2 seconds) back to the near object. Each time the object and pencil should be seen clearly in focus.

4. Repeat the above procedures for a total of 10 cycles or 20 changes.

5. Have the child cover the left eye with left hand and hold the pencil with the right hand. The pencil should be directly in front of her nose at a distance of 4˝ - 6˝ and clearly in focus.

6. Have the child look quickly (about 2 seconds) to a picture, clock or chair across the room, and then quickly (about 2 seconds) back to the near object. Each time the object and pencil should be seen clearly in focus.

7. Repeat the procedures for a total of 10 cycles or 20 changes.

⚠ The technique should be done with one eye at a time, but not both eyes together.

The teacher should check that the focusing is clear by asking the child to describe details of both near and distance objects.

As child gains speed and fluidity, move the pencil closer to her face.

CORE Vision - Focusing

That's one S.M.A.R.T. Teacher!

🍎 **Freda in Coon Rapids** uses herself as the far target! She tells her children *"Eyes on your thumb"* and then *"Eyes on me"* and she shows them a great smile. It is just one way she knows her children see a smiling face every day. It is also a great way to get their attention later in the day, *"Eyes on me!"*

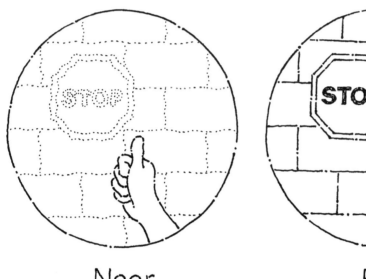

Near
(look at your thumb)

Far
(look at the sign)

LEARNING Stage 1

- The child's eyes may water or she may want to rub them. Continued repetition over time will decrease this response.

WORKING Stage 2

- The child's eyes may over and/or undershoot the "target." Repetition over time, will result in accurate focusing.

GOT IT! Stage 3

- The children are able to shift focus from near to far quickly, accurately and repeatedly for the full duration of the activity.

☺ **Start where the child is at.** For example, if a child is at Stage 2, begin there and progress forward. For more information see page 22.

CORE Vision - Focusing

Putting It All Together

Here's where you

"Start with the CORE before adding MORE."

- *All Through The Day*
- *S.M.A.R.T. Courses*
- *S.M.A.R.T. Themes*

All Through The Day The S.M.A.R.T. Way

Each S.M.A.R.T. Pre-K CORE activity takes just a few minutes to do. They can be done individually throughout the day and/or in combination for a goal of:

- **20 Minutes**
- **Every Day**
- **All Year Through**

© 2011, A Chance To Grow, Inc.

Gross Motor Time

A great time to do a structured S.M.A.R.T. Course! Check the S.M.A.R.T. Courses section on page 93 for ideas.

Warm up activities

- Helicopter Spins
- Superman
- Popcorn
- Stable Table
- Flamingos

Use your existing Gross Motor space as a S.M.A.R.T. Room or if your building has an extra room, create a designated S.M.A.R.T. Room. It is ideal to leave the equipment in place versus having to set up and tear down daily.

If setting up daily is your only option, have confidence you are not alone. Many teachers have done this successfully. Involve the children. They enjoy helping in the set up and tear down.

Switch-a-Roos
(Transitions)

- Balance walk
- Cross Pattern walk
- Free Creep
- Alligator Crawl
- Pencil Roll
- Jumping
- Hopping
- Flower Power
  (Do with an individual child, then dismiss.)
- Helicopter Spins
  (Do with the whole class, 2 - 3 before the transition.)

Circle Time

- Basic Vision (if you can have a room very dark)
- Swinging Ball
- Thumbs Up
- Near/Far Focus
- Stable Table
- Flamingos

Center Time

A great time to do a structured S.M.A.R.T. Course! Check the S.M.A.R.T. Courses section on page 93 for ideas.

Free Creep
Place a tunnel at the entrance of a center. The children creep through the tunnel to enter and exit the center.

Balance Beam
Place a Balance Beam yardstick or line at the entrance of the center. The children do a heel-to-toe walk to enter and exit the center.

Hopscotch
Place a Hopscotch mat at the entrance of center. Children hop into and out of the center.

Helicopter Spins
Use a spin break between centers. Ask the children to stop working and do 2 or 3 Helicopter Spins. Then move to the next center.

Superman or Popcorn
Superman or Popcorn break between centers. Ask the children to stop the activity and do 2 or 3 Supermans or Popcorns. Then move to the next center.

Driver's Ed
Have a variety of street courses on which the children drive little carss.

Magic Erasers
As a center activity at the board or table.

Overs and Unders
Have several variations as a center activity at a table for the children to use.

Loop de Loos
Have several variations as a center activity at a table for the children to use.

Tactile Trackers
Post a few Tactile Trackers near or in a center. The children trace the tracker before they start the center activity.

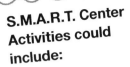

S.M.A.R.T. Center Activities could include:

CORE:
- Rebounder
- Balance Beam
- Hopscotch
- Driver's Ed
- Magic Erasers
- Loop de Loos

Note:
☐ This is a good place to introduce new S.M.A.R.T. Activities to a small group of children if you or an assistant can supervise.

S.M.A.R.T. Courses

We want your children to creep, crawl, roll, spin, balance, jump and hop each day.

Every Pre-K program is different...
different space, schedule, number of children, etc.

So when you begin to develop your S.M.A.R.T. Pre-K program, all those factors need to be taken into consideration. Many teachers prefer to do the S.M.A.R.T. Pre-K Activities in their classrooms. They feel the time is not wasted transitioning the children to a specific S.M.A.R.T. Room. Other teachers prefer to establish a S.M.A.R.T. Room. The equipment can be left out every day so the teachers don't have to set it up and take it down. The next few pages will give you a few suggestions for both approaches.

"We want your children to creep,
crawl, roll, spin, balance, jump
and hop each day."

Setting Up the Course

Having 2 spots for Slap Track and 2 spots for Alligator Crawling in your S.M.A.R.T. Course will increase the frequency, intensity and duration of the vital stimulation these activities provide.

Below is a simple "recipe" for your course:

- 2 Slap Tracks every day all year (switch cards every 2 weeks)
- 2 Alligator Crawls every day, all year
- 1 Balance Beam every day, all year
- 1 More Balance Activity every day, all year (Balance Beam, Flamingos, tape line)
- 1 Pencil Rolls every day, all year
- 1 Rebounder
- 1 Hopscotch mat
- 1 Overhead Ladder, if available

⚠ **Do not place a balance activity after rolling when designing your S.M.A.R.T. Course.**

Choose an area for S.M.A.R.T. Pre-K that works for you!

Here are a few tips that you may want to keep in mind as you set up your S.M.A.R.T. Program:

Classroom Approach

- Train the children to set up and take down the equipment.
- Place the equipment around the perimeter of the classroom.
- Place the equipment in a circuit formation.
- Use your group-time rug. It may be the perfect place for Pencil Rolls.
- The natural walkway areas of the room should be used.
- If you have an area with linoleum flooring, use it for Alligator Crawls.

S.M.A.R.T. Room Approach

- Establish a daily schedule if more than one class is using the S.M.A.R.T Room.
- Establish a weekly or bi-weekly schedule to decide which teacher is in charge of maintaining the room and making changes or variations to the S.M.A.R.T Course.
- Notify custodial staff to make sure the room is vacuumed and cleaned daily.
- Train the children to straighten the last activity area they use before leaving the S.M.A.R.T Room. *"Get the room ready for company."*

Hallway Approach

- Train the children to set up and take down the equipment.
- Place the equipment down the hallway in a long circuit.
- Establish a schedule for the use of the hallway if more than one class is involved.

Note:

☐ **Make it your own.** What works one year may not the next. The same can be true with groups of children. What works with the morning group may not with the afternoon group.

We recommend the 'Divide and Conquer Method'

Based on the experience of the Pre-K teachers we've worked with, we recommend this method. It works well with the Classroom, S.M.A.R.T. Room or Hallway Approaches listed on the previous page. Part of the class rotates through the S.M.A.R.T. Activities, while the rest of the class is working at their tables or in another part of the classroom. Depending on the children's maturity, your class size and schedule, we recommend that you divide your class in half. (Some teachers even have divided their class into thirds!)

Each group needs 1 or 2 adults to supervise.
- Group 1 starts on the S.M.A.R.T. Course while Group 2 is at the tables or in another part of the classroom.
- After Group 1 completes 4 - 5 laps around the course, they change places with Group 2.
- Then Group 2 does the S.M.A.R.T. Course while Group 1 works at the tables or in another part of the classroom.

Activities the children can do when not doing the S.M.A.R.T. Course:

CORE Activities
- Tactile Trackers
- Flower Power
- Driver's Ed
- Magic Erasers
- Loop de Loos
- Overs and Unders
- Basic Vision

MORE ACTIVITIES can be found in **Get to the MORE of Readiness,** the CORE companion book. Available from www.actg.org/smartprek

MORE Activities
- Learning Ladders
- Rainbow Tracing
- Fine Motor Activities

S.M.A.R.T. Room Course — 2-minute stations
Divide and Conquer - "Up and Down"

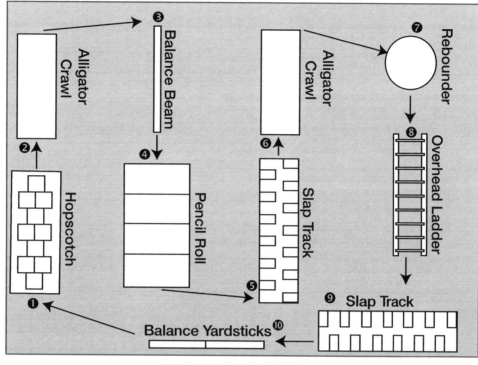

Do not have children balance after rolling.

Each station is 2 minutes.

TEACHER TOOLBOX

- 2 vinyl carpet runners or mats or linoleum floor for Alligator Crawls
- 2 Slap Tracks
- 1 Balance Beam
- 2 - 3 Balance Yardsticks with Velcro on bottom to connect and secure
- 1 Rebounder
- 1 Hopscotch mat
- 1 Overhead Ladder (Slap Track or Alligator Crawl can be substituted)
- Painter's tape (to show where shoulders should be for Pencil Rolls)
- Kitchen timer

How to set up

1. Lay out equipment into 4 columns.
2. Place directional arrows on the floor with painter's tape.
3. Label the stations with numbers, letters or animals, etc.
4. Divide the children into two groups. Group 1 does the S.M.A.R.T. stations and Group 2 does an activity in the classroom. See page 96 for a list of activities.
5. Using Group 1 have one child start at each station.
6. Set the timer for 2 minutes for each station.
7. When the timer goes off, have the children stop, get into a ready position and point to their next station.
8. Have the children do a S.M.A.R.T. transition movement to next station, i.e. Cross Pattern walk, Balance walk, Free Creep, etc.
9. After Group 1 has rotated to all the S.M.A.R.T. stations, switch groups and repeat with Group 2.

Note: If you have a small class size, (10 - 12) and two or three adults to supervise the activities, you can have two children start at each station and do the whole class at one time.

S.M.A.R.T. Room Course — 2-minute stations
Divide and Conquer - "Round We Go"

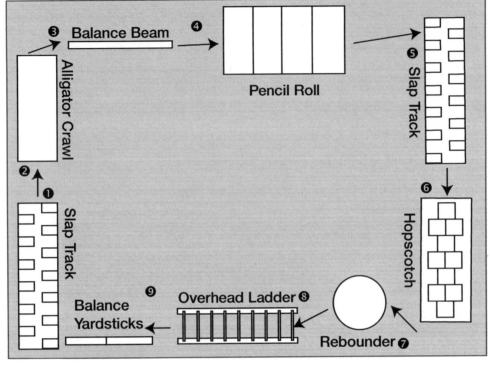

Each station is 2 minutes.

STOP — Do not have children balance after rolling.

TEACHER TOOLBOX

- 1 vinyl carpet runner or mat or linoleum floor for Alligator Crawl
- 2 Slap Tracks
- 1 Balance Beam
- 2 - 3 Balance Yardsticks with Velcro on bottom to connect and secure
- 1 Rebounder
- 1 Hopscotch mat
- 1 Overhead Ladder (Alligator Crawl can be substituted)
- Painter's tape (to show where shoulders should be for Pencil Rolls)
- Kitchen timer

How to set up

1. Lay out equipment around the perimeter of the room.
2. Place directional arrows on the floor with painter's tape.
3. Label the stations with numbers, letters or animals, etc.
4. Divide the children into two groups. Group 1 does the S.M.A.R.T. stations and Group 2 does an activity in the classroom. See page 96 for a list of activities.
5. Using Group 1 have one child start at each piece of equipment.
6. Set the timer for 2 minutes for each station.
7. When the timer goes off, have the children stop, get into a ready position and point to their next station.
8. Have the children do a S.M.A.R.T. transition movement to next station, i.e. Cross Pattern walk, Balance walk, Free Creep, etc.
9. After Group 1 has rotated to all the S.M.A.R.T. stations, switch groups and repeat with Group 2.

Note: If you have a small class size, (10 - 12) and two or three adults to supervise the activities, you can have two children start at each station and do the whole class at one time.

S.M.A.R.T. Room Course — Continuous Laps
Divide and Conquer - "Laughter and Laps"

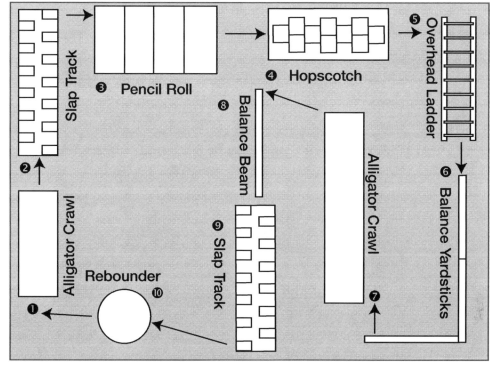

Do not have children balance after rolling.

TEACHER TOOLBOX

- 2 vinyl carpet runners or mats or linoleum floor for Alligator Crawl
- 2 Slap Tracks
- 1 Balance Beam
- 2 - 3 Balance Yardsticks with Velcro on bottom to connect and secure

- 1 Rebounder
- 1 Hopscotch mat
- 1 Overhead Ladder (Slap Track or Alligator Crawl can be substituted)
- Painter's tape (to show where shoulders should be for Pencil Rolls)

How to set up

1. Lay out equipment in an obstacle course.
2. Place directional arrows on the floor with painter's tape.
3. Label the stations with numbers, letters or animals, etc.
4. Divide the children into two groups. Group 1 does the S.M.A.R.T. stations and Group 2 does an activity in the classroom. See page 96 for a list of activities.
5. Using Group 1 have one child start at each piece of equipment.
6. The children rotate continuously around the room (4 - 5 laps).
7. After Group 1 has rotated to all the S.M.A.R.T. stations, switch groups and repeat with Group 2.

 Establish a *"No passing the person in front of you"* rule.

Note: If you have a small class size, (10 - 12) and two or three adults to supervise the activities, you can have two children start at each station and do the whole class at one time.

© 2011, A Chance To Grow, Inc.

S.M.A.R.T. Course In Classroom — 2-minute stations
Divide and Conquer - "Ring Around the Classroom"

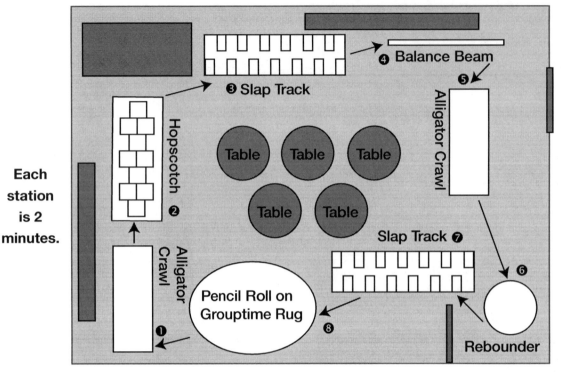

Each station is 2 minutes.

Do not have children balance after rolling.

TEACHER TOOLBOX

- 2 vinyl carpet runners or mats or linoleum floor for Alligator Crawls
- 2 Slap Tracks
- 1 Balance Beam
- 1 Rebounder
- 1 Hopscotch mat
- Painter's tape (to show where shoulders should be for Pencil Rolls)
- Kitchen timer

How to set up

1. Lay out equipment into a circle around the classroom.
2. Place directional arrows on the floor with painter's tape.
3. Label the stations with numbers, letters or animals, etc.
4. Divide the children into two groups. Group 1 does the S.M.A.R.T. stations and Group 2 does an activity at the tables. See page 96 for a list of activities. (One adult supervises the tables and one or two adults supervise the S.M.A.R.T. Course.)
5. Using Group 1 have one child start at each piece of equipment.
6. Set the timer for 2 minutes for each station.
7. When timer goes off, have the children stop, get into a ready position and point to their next station.
8. Have the children do a S.M.A.R.T. transition movement to next station, i.e. Cross Pattern walk, Balance walk, Free Creep, etc.
9. After Group 1 has rotated to all the S.M.A.R.T. stations, switch groups and repeat with Group 2.

S.M.A.R.T. Course In Classroom — Continuous Laps
Divide and Conquer - "Wiggle Room"

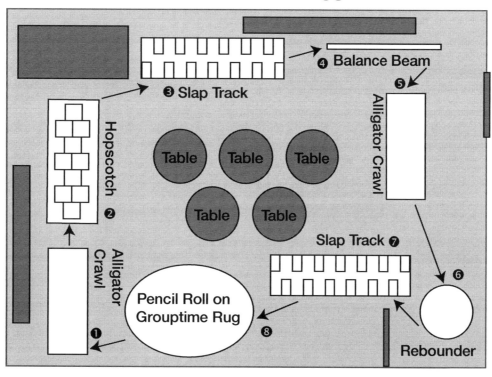

Do not have children balance after rolling.

TEACHER TOOLBOX

- 2 vinyl carpet runners or mats or linoleum floor for Alligator Crawls
- 2 Slap Tracks
- 1 Balance Beam
- 1 Rebounder
- 1 Hopscotch mat
- Painter's tape (to show where shoulders should be for Pencil Rolls)

How to set up

1. Lay out equipment in a circle around the classroom.
2. Place directional arrows on the floor with painter's tape.
3. Label the stations with numbers, letters or animals, etc.
4. Divide the children into two groups. Group 1 does the S.M.A.R.T. stations and Group 2 does an activity at the tables. See page 96 for a list of activities. (One adult supervises the tables and one or two adults supervise the S.M.A.R.T. Course.)
5. Using Group 1 have one child start at each piece of equipment.
6. The children rotate continuously around the room (4 - 5 laps).
7. After Group 1 has rotated to all the S.M.A.R.T. stations, switch groups and repeat with Group 2.

 Establish a *"No passing the person in front of you"* rule.

Note: If you have a small class size, (10 - 12) and two or three adults to supervise the activities, you can have two children start at each station and do the whole class at one time.

© 2011, A Chance To Grow, Inc.   S.M.A.R.T. Pre-K CORE Program Guide • 101

S.M.A.R.T. Course In Hallway
Divide and Conquer - "Just Passing Through"

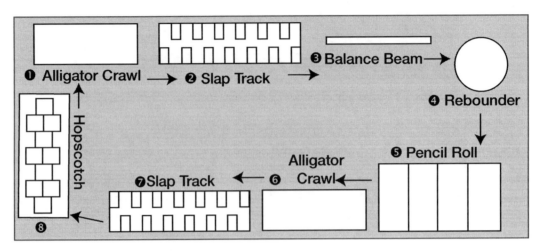

 Do not have children balance after rolling.

 Beware of door placement.

• • • • • • • • • • • **TEACHER TOOLBOX** • • • • • • • • • • •

- 2 vinyl carpet runners or mats or linoleum floor for Alligator Crawls
- 2 Slap Tracks
- 1 Balance Beam
- 1 Rebounder
- 1 Hopscotch mat
- Painter's tape (to show where shoulders should be for Pencil Rolls)

How to set up

1. Lay out equipment in a long circuit in the hallway (take note of location of any doors).
2. Place directional arrows on the floor with painter's tape.
3. Label the stations with numbers, letters or animals, etc.
4. Divide the children into two groups. Group 1 does the S.M.A.R.T. stations and Group 2 does an activity in the classroom. See page 96 for a list of activities.
5. Using Group 1 have one child start at each piece of equipment.
6. After Group 1 has completed the 4 - 5 laps of the hallway course switch groups and repeat with Group 2.

 This is a small course.

It may be necessary to divide your class into three groups and rotate all three groups through the course.

S.M.A.R.T. Themes

Using themes is a great way to keep the same activities exciting and fun. Here are four creative themes your children are sure to enjoy!

Awesome Autumn

Alligator Crawling:

- **Crawl through the Leaves** Hang plastic or construction paper leaves on a baton or stick that is taped to 2 cones. The children crawl under the baton.
  OR
  Place colorful construction paper leaves under the vinyl carpet runner.

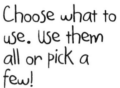

Choose what to use. Use them all or pick a few!

Overhead Ladder:

- **Falling Leaves** Hang large construction paper leaves from the rungs on the Overhead Ladder with letters or numbers to review. The children say the letters or numbers as they cross the ladder.

Slap Track:

- **Vocabulary**
  Put autumn color cards in the Slap Track.
  Example: red, gold, brown, red, gold, brown—Repeat.
  (Write "red" in red marker, "brown" in brown marker, etc.)

  ⚠ Only only 2 or 3 different cards.

- **Fall Cards**
  Put fall words cards with a picture in the Slap Track
  Example: brown, nut, brown, nut—Repeat.
  gold, leaf, gold, leaf—Repeat.
  red, coat, red, coat—Repeat.

  ⚠ Only use a maximum of 4 different cards.

- **Counting**
  Put cards with a picture to represent concepts of quantity in the Slap Track.
  Example: 1 squirrel, 2 pumpkins, 3 leaves
  Write the numeral under the picture.
  The children say the numerals 1, 2, 3, 1, 2, 3—Repeat.

  ⚠ Only use a maximum of 4 different cards.

Balance Beam:

Scatter construction paper leaves under the Balance Beam.

- **Step Over** Place a mini pumpkin, gourd or Indian corn on the Balance Beam for the children to step over. (Choose just 1 "step-over" so the children can still do a heel-to-toe walk.)

Pencil Rolling:

- **Leaf Roll** Make a variety of large construction paper leaves. Tape or lay them on the rolling area. The children roll over the leaves. Plastic leaves work well too.
  OR
  The children hold a bouquet of plastic leaves over their heads as they roll.

Rebounder:

- **Learning Ladders** from <u>**S.M.A.R.T. Pre-K Get to the MORE of Readiness**</u>. The children jump and say the information on the Learning Ladders. Use fall colors and vocabulary.

Overs and Unders:

- **Pumpkins and Cornstalks** Create an Overs and Unders sheet using pumpkin and cornstalk clip art. Have the children trace over the cornstalks and under the pumpkins.

Tactile Trackers:

- **Oh Nuts!** Draw 4 squirrels on the left side of the Tactile Tracker. Draw 4 acorns on the right side of the Tactile Tracker. Connect the squirrels to the nuts with curvy, random lines. Use a different color for each line. The children should trace the line from the squirrel to the correct nut. Remind the children to cover left eye and trace. Cover right eye and trace. Trace with both eyes.

- **Leaf Lines** The children can trace the outlines of various fall leaves. Make it tactile by streaming a line of glue on the outline of the leaf.

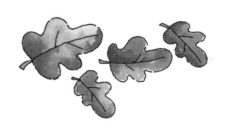

Fabulous Food

Alligator Crawling:

- **Strawberry Patch** Hang plastic berries on a baton or stick that is taped to 2 cones. The children crawl under the baton.

  OR

  Place colorful construction paper strawberries under the vinyl carpet runner.

Overhead Ladder:

- **Crazy Carrots** Hang large construction paper carrots from rungs on the Overhead Ladder with letters or numbers to review. The children say the letters or numbers as they cross the ladder.

Slap Track:

- **Vocabulary** Put food word cards with a picture in the Slap Track.
  Example: beans, corn, rice, beans, corn, rice—Repeat.
  ⚠ Only use a maximum of 4 different cards.

- **Rhyming** Put rhyming words with pictures in a repeating pattern in the Slap Track.
  Example: eat, meat, eat, meat—Repeat.
  green, beans, green, beans—Repeat.
  ⚠ Only use a maximum of 4 different cards.

- **Simple Sentences** I like peas. Include a picture with the word—peas.
  I like milk. Include picture with the word—milk.
  Repeat the sentence the full length of the Slap Track.

- **Counting** Put cards with fruits and vegetables to represent concepts of quantity in the Slap Track. Write the numeral under the picture. The children say the numeral.
  Example: 3 bananas, 5 apples, 7 plums—Repeat.
  ⚠ Only use a maximum of 4 different cards.

Choose what to use.
Use them all or pick a few!

Balance Beam:

- **"Got Milk?"** Place empty, cleaned milk cartons on the Balance Beam for the children to step over. (Use just 2 "step-overs" so the children can still do a heel-to-toe walk.)

- **Mixing Bowl** Place a hoop taped on onto 2 cones above the Balance Beam. The children step into and out of the "mixing bowl" as they walk the Balance Beam.

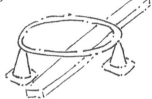

- **Food Basket** Place baskets of plastic food at the beginning and end of the Balance Beam. The children pick up a piece of plastic food and carry it as they do a heel-to-toe walk. When they get to the end of the beam they drop the fruit into the second basket.

Hopscotch:

- **Hot Griddle Jump** The children pretend the Hopscotch rug is a hot griddle. They need to jump quickly across the rug or Hopscotch pattern on the floor.

Pencil Rolling:

- **Fruit Salad** Place photographs of a variety of fruit on the area where the children roll. They roll over the "fruit salad."

- **Mashed Potatoes** Place construction paper potatoes on the rolling area. The children hold a potato masher as they roll over the potatoes to "mash" them.

Rebounder:

- **Learning Ladders** from <u>S.M.A.R.T. Pre-K Get to the MORE of Readiness.</u> The children jump and say the information on the Learning Ladders. Use alliterative food words.

- **Alliterative Food Words** Tape a letter and 3 pictures of words that begin with that letter on the wall. The children jump and say the letter and the 3 pictures. The pictures can also have the word written below it.
  Example: B-bread, butter, beans
  　　　　　R-rice, raspberries, rutabagas

Tactile Trackers:

- **Play with Your Food** The children can trace the outlines of various foods. You can use actual photos that are large enough to place on the wall or create simple designs on poster board. Remember to add something to make them tactile.

© 2011, A Chance To Grow, Inc.　　S.M.A.R.T. Pre-K CORE Program Guide • 107

Things That Go

Alligator Crawling:

- **Car Wash** Hang steamers on a baton or stick that is taped to 2 cones. The children crawl under the baton and through the streamers.

- **Honk Your Horn** When the children crawl all the way to the "finish line" they get to honk a bike horn. A hotel bell, drum, tambourine, squeaky dog toy could be used.

Overhead Ladder:

- **Flying High** Hang large construction paper airplanes, hot air balloons or helicopters from the rungs on the Overhead Ladder with letters or numbers to review. The children say the letters or numbers as they cross the ladder.

Slap Track:

- **Vocabulary** Cut out shapes of a boat on a white piece of construction paper. Write simple vocabulary words and put them in the Slap Track.
  Example: big, boat, big, boat—Repeat.
  go, slow, go, slow—Repeat.
  ⚠ Only use a maximum of 2 different cards.

- **Vocabulary Cards** Put words with a picture in a repeating pattern in the Slap Track.
  Example: red, boat, blue, sea, red, boat, blue, sea—Repeat.
  ⚠ Only use a maximum of 4 different cards.

- **Counting** Put cards with picture to represent concepts of quantity.
  Example: 4 boats, 5 planes, 6 cars
  Write the numeral under the picture.
  The children say the numeral. 4, 5, 6, 4, 5, 6—Repeat.
  When the children are confident with saying the numerals, you can rearrange the order in a different repeating pattern. 6, 4, 5, 6, 4, 5—Repeat.
  ⚠ Only use a maximum of 4 different cards.

Choose what to use. Use them all or pick a few!

Balance Beam:

- **Car Lot** Place 1 or 2 small plastic cars on the Balance Beam. The children step over the cars as they do a heel-to-toe walk.

- **Back Up the Truck** The children "put themselves in reverse" and do a backwards toe-to-heel walk on the beam.

Pencil Rolling:

- **Steam Roller** Lay a variety of soft objects (stuffed toys, socks, mittens, etc.) on the rolling area. The children are "steam rollers" and roll over the objects.

- **Speed Bump** Place a pool noodle under the mat, long rug or a piece of vinyl carpet runner. The children roll over the "speed bump."

Overs and Unders:

- **Airplanes and Submarines** Create an Overs and Unders sheet using airplanes and submarines. Have the children trace over the airplanes and under the submarines.

Rebounder:

- **Learning Ladders** from *S.M.A.R.T. Pre-K Get to the MORE of Readiness* The children jump and say the information on the Learning Ladders.

- **Make Car, Boat and Plane Die Cuts.** Write letters or numbers on them or simply make them from different colors of paper. Create the Learning Ladders from these die cuts.

Driver's Ed:

- **Driving You Crazy** Create several different types of roads (race tracks, dirt roads, monster truck trails) for the children to practice their driving skills.

Tactile Trackers:

- **Fun Flyers** Draw 4 airplanes on the left side of the Tactile Tracker. Draw 4 hangars on the right side of the Tactile Tracker. Connect the airplanes to the hangars with curvy, random lines. Use different colors for each. The children trace the line from the airplane to the correct hangar. Remind the children to cover left eye and trace. Cover right eye and trace. Trace with both eyes.

Bugs Bugs Bugs

Alligator Crawling:

- **Bug Crawl** Hang plastic bugs on a baton or stick that is taped to 2 cones. The children crawl under the baton.
  OR
  Place colorful construction paper bugs under the vinyl carpet runner.

Overhead Ladder:

- **Buzz a Rung** Hang large construction paper bumblebees from the rungs on the Overhead Ladder with letters or numbers to review. The children say the letters or numbers as they cross the ladder.

Choose what to use. Use them all or pick a few!

Slap Track:

- **Vocabulary** Put bug word cards with a picture in the Slap Track.
  Example: bee, fly, ant, bee, fly, ant, bee, fly, ant—Repeat.
  ⚠ Only use a maximum of 4 different cards.

- **Rhyming** Put rhyming word cards in a repeating pattern in the Slap Track.
  Example: bug, rug, mug, bug, rug, mug—Repeat.
  ⚠ Only use a maximum of 4 different cards.

- **Counting** Put cards with bees and bugs to represent concepts of quantity in the Slap Track. Write the numeral under the picture. The children say the numeral.
  Example: 2 bees, 4 ants, 6 bugs—Repeat.
  ⚠ Only use a maximum of 4 different cards.

Balance Beam:

- **The Bees Knees** Tape construction bees on 1 or 2 plastic cups. Place bee cups on the Balance Beam for children to step over. (Choose just 2 "step-overs" so the children can still do a heel-to-toe walk.)

Pencil Rolling:

- **Bug Roll** Make a variety of large construction paper bugs. Tape or lay them on the rolling mat or area. The children roll over the bugs to "squish" them.

- **Worm Roll** Place plastic worms (fishing lures) on the rolling area. The children roll over the "squishy worms."

Overs and Unders:

- **Butterflies and Beetles** Create an Overs and Unders sheet using butterflies and beetles clip art. Have the children trace over the butterflies and under the beetles.

Rebounder:

- **Learning Ladders** from <u>S.M.A.R.T. Pre-K Get to the MORE of Readiness.</u> The children jump and say the information on the Learning Ladders. Use alliterative bug words.

- **Alliterative Bug Words** Tape a letter and 3 pictures of alliterative bug words that begin with that letter on the wall. The children jump and say the letter and the 3 pictures. The pictures can also have the word written below it.
  Example: B-bee, bugs, butterfly

Tactile Trackers:

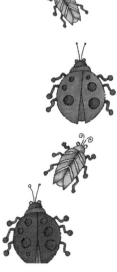

- **Back to the Beehive** Draw 4 bees on the left side of the Tactile Tracker. Draw 4 beehives on the right side of the Tactile Tracker. Connect the bees to the hives with curvy, random lines. Use a different color for each line. The children trace the line from the bee to the correct hive. Remind the children to cover left eye and trace. Cover right eye and trace. Trace with both eyes.

- **Bug Lines** The children can trace the outlines of various bugs, butterflies and bees. You can use actual photos that are large enough to place on the wall or create simple designs on poster board.

Want MORE Themes?

S.M.A.R.T. Pre-K Program Guides:

- **CORE Themes & Masters**
- **MORE Themes & Masters**

A delightful and practical selection of ideas to utilize our Pre-K program all year long for both our Pre-K CORE and MORE Activities. Each book features four fun themes in six categories for a total of 24 exciting themes!

1. Silly Seasons
2. Creatures & Critters
3. Fantastic Folks
4. All About Me
5. Wonderful World
6. Go Go Go

Appendices

APPENDIX A

Letter to Your Families

On the next page you will find a letter to the families of the children in your class. You have permission to copy and distribute the letter, or use it as a guide to craft your own letter. Either way, we suggest you tell the families about the S.M.A.R.T. Pre-K Program and Activities.

Download a printable version: www.actg.org/smartprek

Dear Family,

This year, your child will be participating in an exciting program called S.M.A.R.T. Pre-K which stands for Stimulating Maturity through Accelerated Readiness Training. S.M.A.R.T. Pre-K is a multi-sensory approach to learning for 3 - 5 year olds that involves brain stimulation activities, to help prepare your child to learn. This program develops visual, auditory, balance, fine and gross motor readiness, all required skills essential for classroom and academic success. The S.M.A.R.T. Pre-K Activities also improve your child's physical fitness, strength, coordination and ability to pay attention. Once these readiness skills are in place, your child will have the foundation necessary to succeed in school.

S.M.A.R.T. Pre-K Activities involve a number of purposeful exercises, including:

- Crawling
- Creeping
- Spinning
- Balancing
- Rolling
- Overhead Ladder

The S.M.A.R.T. Pre-K Activities will be integrated into the daily classroom schedule in a fun and positive way to help your child reach his/her learning potential. If you have any questions, please do not hesitate to contact me.

Sincerely,

Your Child's Teacher

APPENDIX B

About A Chance To Grow

A Chance To Grow was founded in 1985 by Bob and Kathy DeBoer and a group of parents looking for a better chance at success for their children with serious brain injuries and developmental delays. Since then, the agency has grown to include a continuum of services for *all children*, ranging from those having difficulty learning to read through those with problems as challenging as autism, cerebral palsy or coma. Our latest work adds the Pre-K component, allowing us to be proactive in helping prepare children to learn prior to their entry into school.

Our "product" is better children, equipped with the skills needed to lead them toward independence and success. An autistic child needs help integrating information coming in through her senses. A pre-schooler may need help learning to spin and roll, activities that will help her better attend. And a failing reader in second grade often needs help developing pre-reading skills so she can learn to read without struggling.

A Chance To Grow specialists use an interdisciplinary approach and the latest brain research to develop a continuum of programs for children, ranging from educational programs to specialty clinics to rehabilitation services. All of our programs take each child's unique needs and abilities into account. Our services are specifically tailored to the individual child to ensure that she reaches her highest potential.

With that as our goal, A Chance To Grow has developed a variety of interventions and educational offerings for educators, parents and other professionals. While S.M.A.R.T. at the elementary level and now S.M.A.R.T. Pre-K for three to five-year olds can be applied systemically, helping all children succeed within the classroom, other interventions are also available for those children who may need additional intervention.

These interventions include Audio Visual Entrainment (AVE), Hemisphere Specific Auditory Stimulation (HSAS) — both offered at A Chance To Grow as well as in a workshop format for families and educators. Additional workshops offered include Fairmont Reading Assessment Program (FRAP) and Dyslexia Program Teaching. For families looking for an intensive, out-of-school option for their children, Summer Boost Up Plus at A Chance To Grow is yet another option.

A Chance To Grow and the MLRC offer additional interventions for addressing more specific developmental issues

The Minnesota Learning Resource Center (MLRC) is a program of A Chance To Grow, and serves as the agency's teacher training institute, helping to replicate ACTG within schools and other organizations. The MLRC was established through funding by the state legislature and its model is to present information through a variety of workshops and provide follow-up, on-site mentoring to assist in program implementation. The MLRC led the S.M.A.R.T. – Early Childhood Project, resulting in the S.M.A.R.T. Pre-K Program Guide and workshop.

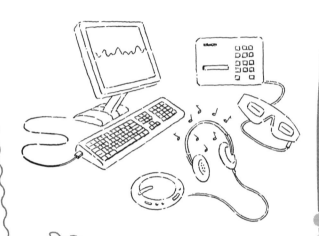

HSAS

Hemisphere Specific Auditory Stimulation (HSAS) uses individualized music compact discs, based on the results of an audiogram or hearing test, to stimulate the brain and develop the auditory pathways. It is designed to shape an optimal hearing curve and right ear dominance, which is shown to be critical to listening and understanding language.

For more information, please contact the MLRC: 612-706-5549 or mlrc@actg.org

AVE

Audio Visual Entrainment (AVE) is a technology that uses the brain's natural tendency to follow light and sound to reinforce healthy brain wave patterns and improve functionality. It involves the use of a small music device, headphones, "light" glasses and tones that can be useful for concerns with learning disabilities, behavioral and/or emotional disorders.

For more information, please contact the MLRC: 612-706-5549 or mlrc@actg.org

We offer workshops and training to provide even MORE fun information in working with brain stimulation and children.

Summer Boost Up Plus

Summer Boost Up Plus is a fun and multi-sensory program for kids. It combines the benefits of S.M.A.R.T. and other A Chance To Grow interventions into daily activities over a three-week period. During this time, each child receives Boost Up (S.M.A.R.T.) as well as auditory processing, EEG Biofeedback, Audio Visual Entrainment, fine motor/arts & crafts and yoga activities. Individualized Vision Therapy may also be available. Summer Boost Up Plus is offered at A Chance To Grow in northeast Minneapolis.

For more information, please contact Rehabilitation Services: 612-746-5140 or boostupplus@actg.org

Dyslexia

The **Introduction to Dyslexia Program Teaching** workshop utilizes concepts and techniques from three proven methods:

(1) Motor planning and laterality to improve fundamental readiness skills;

(2) Halapin Letter Dynamics for the development of concrete written principles; and

(3) Multisensory Language Therapy for irregular phoneme patterns.

For workshop nformation, please contact the MLRC: 612-706-5549 or mlrc@actg.org

FRAP

The **Fairmont Reading Acceleration Program** (FRAP), workshop is an extension of S.M.A.R.T. and demonstrates how to assess and accelerate students' reading achievement. The workshop teaches educators how the brain learns to read, how to respond to specific areas of weakness and how to match interventions to learner characteristics.

For workshop information, please contact the MLRC: 612-706-5549 or mlrc@actg.org

APPENDIX C

S.M.A.R.T.– Early Childhood* Project: Executive Summary

Over the past decade and a half, ACTG has worked with elementary school teachers to introduce the S.M.A.R.T. Program (Stimulating Maturity through Accelerated Readiness Training) into elementary school daily instruction. From 2005-2010, A Chance To Grow piloted the S.M.A.R.T – E.C. Program. S.M.A.R.T. – E.C. is a program that uses brain stimulation exercises to help low-income children become ready for kindergarten. Prepared by Gary Miller Consulting. Gary Miller, Ph.D., Carl Franzen, Jeanette Lieberman, Colleen McLaughlin

* Originally, The S.M.A.R.T. Pre-K program was called S.M.A.R.T. – Early Childhood or S.M.A.R.T. – E.C. For purposes of this report, the program will be referred to as S.M.A.R.T. – E.C..

History

A Chance To Grow (ACTG) promotes the maximum development of the whole child through innovative, individualized and comprehensive brain-centered programs and services. These services are educational, therapeutic and rehabilitative in nature. Over the past decade and a half, ACTG has worked with elementary school teachers to introduce the S.M.A.R.T. curriculum (Stimulating Maturity through Accelerated Readiness Training) into elementary school daily instruction. The S.M.A.R.T. curriculum provides brain stimulation for improved learning readiness, literacy and math skills. ACTG has trained over 4,000 teachers in twelve states.

In 2005, ACTG decided to apply its brain stimulation program to younger children. ACTG partnered with two Head Start programs (in northwest Minnesota and in the Twin City metropolitan area) involving over 20 Head Start classrooms (exact number varied by year). S.M.A.R.T. – E.C. (Stimulating Maturity through Accelerated Readiness Training—Early Childhood) was a six year demonstration project to test the effectiveness of S.M.A.R.T. – E.C. with younger children in preschool settings. This project assumed that pre-school brain stimulation training should be even more effective because of greater brain plasticity in the earlier years.

Importance of Early Childhood Education

S.M.A.R.T. – E.C. is a demonstration program that uses brain stimulation exercises to help children become ready for kindergarten. Too many children are arriving at kindergarten and grade school unprepared to learn and lacking skills needed in order to learn to read, such as listening and vocabulary skills, visual perception, eye-hand coordination, social interaction patterns, attention to following directions, pencil-paper skills, gross and fine motor skills and self-confidence in the face of challenges.

- In a ground-breaking study, Hart and Risley (1995) found that while some children enter kindergarten with a vocabulary of 4,000 words, children from deprived environments in the same class may only know 2,000 words.
- Roughly half of children entering Minnesota kindergartens were not proficient in language/literacy and mathematical thinking (Minnesota School Readiness Business Advisory Council, Ready for School, 2004).
- Another analysis found that children entering kindergarten from lower income families and with parents with less education were significantly more likely than children from higher incomes and with parents with more education to be rated not proficient in language/literacy and mathematical thinking (Minnesota School Readiness Study, 2004).

Poverty and Brain Functioning

S.M.A.R.T. – E.C. is designed to improve brain functioning for children and to encourage educators to bring brain stimulation into the classroom. Recent research has demonstrated a direct relationship between poverty and brain functioning. Researchers at the University of California found that the brains of low-income children function differently than the brains of high-income children. Normal 9- and 10-year old children differing only in socioeconomic status have detectable differences as measured by EEGs in the responses of their prefrontal cortex—the part of the brain critical for problem-solving and creativity. Children from lower socioeconomic levels show brain physiology patterns similar to adults with damage in the frontal lobe (University of California Press Release, 12/2/08).

> "...chronic stress found in many families living in poverty creates a cumulative effect on developing brains..."

The cost of chronic stress found in many families living in poverty creates a cumulative effect on developing brains. The prefrontal cortex and the hippocampus (crucial for learning, cognition, and working memory) are brain areas most affected by cortisol, the "stress hormone." Experiments have demonstrated that exposure to chronic and acute stress shrinks neurons in the brain's frontal lobes affecting making judgments, planning and regulating impulsivity (Cook and Willman, 2004) and can modify or impair the hippocampus in ways that reduce learning capacity (Vythilingam, et. al., 2002).

S.M.A.R.T. – E.C. Design

S.M.A.R.T. – E.C. has four basic components:

- **S.M.A.R.T. – E.C. Curriculum.** The S.M.A.R.T. – E.C. curriculum was used in the classrooms by Head Start staff on a daily basis—15-20 minutes per day. The curriculum involves the children in a series of exercises doing large motor exercises, fine motor activities and vision activities—designed to improve hand/eye coordination, focusing, gross and fine motor skills, sequencing, left/right awareness and spatial relations.
- **Staff Training Workshops.** Prior to the first year of implementation, Head Start teachers and assistants/aides attended a 2½-day workshop on S.M.A.R.T. – E.C., including suggestions on how to adapt it to normal classroom routines, shortened school days and space limitations.
- **Implementation in the Head Start Classrooms.** Teachers and assistants/aides integrated S.M.A.R.T. into their daily schedules.
- **On-going Mentoring of Head Start Staff.** On a regular basis, ACTG mentors visited the Head Start Centers to provide monitoring of implementation, as well as on-going mentoring.

S.M.A.R.T. E.C. Implementation

Since its early beginnings in the 1980s, ACTG has developed new approaches to rehabilitation and learning readiness by first running demonstration projects and then by testing them for effectiveness. ACTG used this same approach with S.M.A.R.T. – E.C. in Head Start sites—first demonstrating, then testing and then disseminating. Years One through Four were devoted to testing the effectiveness of S.M.A.R.T. – E.C., comparing the literacy and learning readiness measures of Head Start children in S.M.A.R.T. – E.C. classrooms with Head Start children in classrooms that did not receive S.M.A.R.T. – E.C.

"After the initial five years of testing, the evidence is clear that S.M.A.R.T. – E.C. has a positive effect on early cognitive development and prepares children for entry into kindergarten..."

After the initial five years of testing, the evidence was clear that S.M.A.R.T. – E.C. has a positive effect on early cognitive development and prepares children for entry into kindergarten. Moreover, the evidence for a positive effect of S.M.A.R.T. – E.C. on early literacy skills and learning readiness got stronger from Years One through Four, reflecting the increased teacher skill and support for the intervention:

Year One: Implementation

Year One was an implementation year in which details of integrating S.M.A.R.T. into a Head Start structure were worked out. The S.M.A.R.T. curriculum was modified to make appropriate for younger children. At both the northwestern Minnesota and metropolitan sites, the first year of implementation was difficult, as teachers had to learn a new technique, work out problems and coordinate across centers. The first year experience underscored the importance of the mentoring of Head Start staff, as individual variability was greater than anticipated.

Years Two to Four: Testing the S.M.A.R.T. Intervention at Head Start Center.

Years Two through Four were demonstration years and involved the testing of the S.M.A.R.T. intervention using two standard tests of early literacy skills and school readiness—IGDI (Individual Growth and Development Indicators) and Brigance K & 1 Screen II (a test of various aspects of school readiness).

- **Year Two.** Test score analysis in Year Two were confined to Head Start centers in the northwestern Minnesota sites, since the metropolitan site was still in its first year of implementation. In this site, Head Start students in S.M.A.R.T. – E.C. classrooms scored higher than students in comparison classrooms—picture naming (some inconsistency), rhyming, alliteration and school readiness. Teacher acceptance of the new tool continued to increase.

- **Year Three.** The third year testing results were mixed and somewhat contradictory and unable to support the hypothesis of greater performance among S.M.A.R.T. – E.C. students. In probing for a deeper understanding, we examined performance gains for just students in full-day, full-year Head Start centers (assuming a longer and more intensive intervention). Over the course of the year, S.M.A.R.T. – E.C. students performed increasingly better in rhyming and alliteration and the same on picture naming (a less demanding test). However, teacher acceptance and evaluation of S.M.A.R.T. – E.C. continued to increase.

- **Year Four.** By the fourth year, a clear pattern had emerged—Head Start children who received S.M.A.R.T. – E.C. performed better on a variety of tests of early literacy and school readiness than Head Start children who did not receive it. Head Start children who received it performed better on a majority of learning readiness and early literacy tests.

    - In six out of eight comparisons of classrooms at both sites, S.M.A.R.T. – E.C. end-of-the-year IGDI test scores were higher than those of comparison classrooms.
    - In 5 out of 6 comparisons of Fall to Spring improvement scores on IGDI, S.M.A.R.T. – E.C. children performed better than children in comparison classrooms.
    - S.M.A.R.T. – E.C. children's scores for both IGDI and Brigance tests at both sites compared favorably to norms established for five-year olds (a measure of school readiness).

> "By the fourth year, a clear pattern had emerged—Head Start children who received S.M.A.R.T. – E.C. performed better on a variety of tests of early literacy and school readiness…"

Teacher acceptance and enthusiasm for S.M.A.R.T. – E.C. was strong. By the third and fourth years of the demonstration teachers were, by and large, quite enthusiastic about its value and contribution to learning readiness. In fact, teacher praise for S.M.A.R.T. – E.C. was very strong. According to teachers, students in S.M.A.R.T. – E.C. classrooms learned skills faster, focused and concentrated better and learned letters and shapes faster. Teacher comfort with S.M.A.R.T. – E.C. did not become really strong until a long period of trial and error—usually by the end of the second year. By the end of the final year, Head Start teachers at both sites continued to use S.M.A.R.T. – E.C, even though the initial financial support had expired. In addition, S.M.A.R.T. – E.C. has been introduced into other centers that originally served as comparison classrooms.

Following Head Start/S.M.A.R.T. – E.C. Students into Elementary School

Year Five was a follow-up year. By Year Four of the demonstration project, ACTG was ready to follow a subsample of Head Start graduates who had received S.M.A.R.T. – E.C. into elementary school to assess their readiness for school and their early academic skill development. Because of resource and tracking limitations, this follow-up study looked at a smaller sample (N=45) of Head Start/S.M.A.R.T. – E.C. students in elementary school. The follow-up study produced even more positive results.

Year Five.
Tracking Head Start Students into Elementary School

In Year Five (2009-2010), 45 children who received S.M.A.R.T. – E. C. were tracked as they entered elementary school to see how well they performed relative to their classmates and national norms.

Year Five results provide solid evidence that:

- **Head Start/S.M.A.R.T. –** *E.C. students were ready to learn upon entering Kindergarten.*

    Tests of letter naming and sound fluency showed that Head Start/S.M.A.R.T. – E.C. students entered kindergarten scoring very close to the national norms for these tests. These results are encouraging in light of research in Minnesota showing that high percentages of children from low income families enter Kindergarten not proficient in language, literacy and mathematical thinking and significantly higher than higher-income children to be rated not proficient.

- **Head Start/S.M.A.R.T. –** *E.C. students continued to learn at levels expected of all students in subsequent grades.*

    We examined performance of Head Start/S.M.A.R.T. – E.C. students at the end of each of three elementary grades—Kindergarten, First Grade and Second Grade—and compared them with national norms. At all three grade levels, the Head Start/S.M.A.R.T. – E.C. students met or exceeded normative expectations. These are impressive results for low-income students.

There was no evidence of the Head Start fade—*performances at the normative level of Head Start/S.M.A.R.T. – E.C. continued through Grade Two.*

There is always a fear that performance gains in Head Start will fade over time in elementary school. There was no evidence of this in this study. We measured growth scores in reading and math in Grades One and Two and found that Head Start/S.M.A.R.T. – E.C. students improved at the same rate as other students in these grades and at the level of national norms.

Summary

"... evaluation evidence from five years of a six-year demonstration program of S.M.A.R.T. – E.C. ... supports its effectiveness as an early education intervention."

ACTG now has evaluation evidence from five years of a demonstration program of S.M.A.R.T. – E.C. that supports its effectiveness as an early education intervention. Just about everybody with an interest in education deplores existing and persistent achievement gaps between students of varying income levels and racial backgrounds. Yet, little goes beyond describing and deploring the gap. The results of this study suggest that brain-related interventions, especially at an early age, might reduce these nagging inequalities—by elementary school, the Head Start students who received S.M.A.R.T. – E.C. were performing at a level equal to the other elementary school students.

Over the five years, ACTG was able to demonstrate that:

- The S.M.A.R.T. curriculum can be adapted to a preschool setting;
- Teachers can learn, accept, and support this new tool;
- Head Start children receiving S.M.A.R.T. – E.C. generally perform better on tests of early literacy skills and school readiness measures than those who do not receive it;
- Head Start children who received S.M.A.R.T. – E.C. entered kindergarten ready to learn and at a level equal to national norms;
- As Head Start/S.M.A.R.T. – E.C. students progressed through K-2 grades, they continued to learn at levels expected of all students;
- There was no evidence of a "fade" in later grades—the Head Start/S.M.A.R.T. – E.C. students continued to perform at the normative level through Grade 2.

Implications of Research

A number of implications of this research deserve mention:

- It is important to eradicate/reduce inequalities in the early years in order to prevent negative experiences and attitudes from interfering with later learning.
- Getting children ready for school involves more than rehearsing specific behaviors and skills—brain development and stimulation are important tools in getting children ready for school, and once in school, continuing to support learning. S.M.A.R.T. – E.C. addresses an underlying cause of learning deficits rather than addressing a specific learning deficit.
- This research is a reinforcement of the importance of brain-related learning and the need to integrate brain stimulation into the normal educational regimen. Educators shy away from brain issues, as they are not trained in its importance or functioning and many relegate brain development to the medical setting rather than to the classroom. These findings call into question this mindset.
- Even though there is heightened interest in early childhood development, most proposals seldom go beyond calling for more of the same or more funding. S.M.A.R.T. – E.C. provides a promising piece of the puzzle for improving educational outcomes.
- S.M.A.R.T. – E.C. is a relatively inexpensive early childhood intervention. Arthur Rolnick of the Federal Reserve Bank of Minneapolis has championed the advantages of quality early education for poor children and he and other economists have touted the high return on investment of quality early education programs. These return on investment base studies generally used a few Cadillac models, which require very high program investments—at levels seldom found in most early childhood programs. S.M.A.R.T. – E.C., on the other hand, is relatively inexpensive. The up-front costs for teacher training and mentoring are only for 1-3 years and the downstream costs are quite inexpensive.

> "The results of this study suggest that brain-related interventions, especially at an early age, might reduce these nagging inequalities—by elementary school, the Head Start students who received S.M.A.R.T. – E.C. were performing at a level equal to the other elementary school students."

- The introduction of a brain stimulation program in these Head Start centers was continued beyond the period of direct funding and mentoring, as well as was introduced in the remaining centers. In this sense, S.M.A.R.T. – E.C. contributes to the infrastructure development of these preschool settings without any large and ongoing infusion of funding beyond the initial funding for training and mentoring.
- At its heart, S.M.A.R.T. – E.C. and its companion program for elementary school teachers is a teacher training program. Teachers reported how their training for S.M.A.R.T. – E.C., their experiences in using it in their classroom and the ongoing mentoring they received, got them to re-examine their teaching approaches, gave them a better perspective on the relationship between brain development and early childhood education and alerted them to important changes in children's learning, behaviors and school readiness.
- This multi-year evaluation of S.M.A.R.T. – E.C. relied heavily on quantitative, standardized tests of learning readiness, literacy skills and academic progress, namely IGDI and Brigance in the Head Start years and MAP and AIMSweb in the elementary school years. These were demanding tests of learning readiness and skill development. Still more demanding was the use of comparison groups to assess the strength of S.M.A.R.T. – E.C.. Even under these demanding conditions, students receiving S.M.A.R.T. – E.C. performed as or better than expected.
- Finally, the evaluation's reliance on standardized testing should not over-shadow the importance of teacher assessments of the value of S.M.A.R.T. – E.C. and on-site observations of the evaluation staff. Even more importantly, we should acknowledge that this research was not able to document the effects of participation in S.M.A.R.T. – E.C. on children's motivation, attitudes toward learning, self-confidence and impulse control—all factors that we know are related to academic success.

Glossary

Acuity—Sharpness of sight measured with standard 20/20 vision charts.

Alliteration—The repetition of initial consonant sounds in two or more words.

Auditory—Related to or experienced through hearing.

Auditory Closure—The ability to detect the missing speech component of a word or sentence and then fill in the missing information to make the message complete.

Auditory Discrimination—The ability to distinguish the difference between sounds (Example: environmental sounds, phonemes and words).

Auditory Memory—The ability to recall auditory information (Example: environmental sounds, speech sounds, words, numbers, sentences and directions).

Axon—The threadlike part of neuron along which impulses are conducted.

Bilateral Coordination—The ability to use both sides of the body at the same time in a controlled and organized manner.

Brain Stem—The area of the brain, including the Medulla, Pons and Cerebellum or Midbrain, which controls the coordination of all unconscious motor activity.

Crawling—The movement a baby makes when it is on its belly.

Creeping—The movement a baby makes when it is on all fours.

Cortex—The outer layer of the cerebrum, and the area of the brain which controls the coordination of all conscious motor activity.

Dendrite Branching—The inner connections in the brain which make communication between neurons possible.

Directionality—Understanding the concept of up-down, left- right, back-front etc. as projected in space. Laterality, or the knowledge of left and right on oneself, is the basis for directionality.

Duration—The time during which something exists or lasts.

Eye-Hand Coordination—The ability of the eye and hand to work together to complete a task.

Eye Movements—The ability of the eyes to move smoothly from one point to another (Example: Following words on a page from left to right).

Far Point Acuity—Sharpness of vision at 20 feet or chalkboard distance.

Fine Motor—The movements in the hand and wrist muscles requiring a high degree of control and precision.

Focusing—The ability of the eye to focus and quickly change focus from near to far and vice versa.

Frequency—The number of repetitions of a process in a unit of time.

Full Spectrum Music—That which includes a range of high and low frequencies (Example: Orchestral, Classical, Island, Exotic, etc.).

Gross Motor—The movements which involve large muscle groups.

Input—Information offered <u>TO</u> the brain or body.

Intensity—The magnitude of force or energy per unit saturation.

Laterality—The internal awareness of the two sides of the body and their labels of left and right. This serves as a foundation for making directional (left, right) judgments in space (Example: letter reversals).

Mid-line Development—The ability to move one hand, foot, or eye into the space of the other hand, foot or eye.

Multi-Sensory—Ability to stimulate using taste, smell, visual, auditory and tactile pathways.

Myelin—A white fatty sheath around neurons which increases the speed at which impulses are conducted.

Near Point Acuity—Sharpness of vision at 16 inches or reading distance.

Output—Information requested FROM the brain or body.

Physiological—Being in accord with or characteristic of the normal functioning of a living organism.

Proprioception—The ability of the body to know where it is in space (Example: Touch top of head without seeing it).

Readiness Skills—Foundation skills to be able to receive information clearly and consistently through the visual, auditory and tactile pathways.

Sensory Pathways—The routes by which information is conducted to the brain. They include vision, auditory and tactile/kinesthetic.

Sight—The ability to see and the eyes response to light shining into it.

Sound Blending—The ability to hear individual speech sounds (phonemes) and put them together to form a word.

Stimulation—Anything that excites brain activity to increase growth and function.

Tactile—Related to or experience through sense of touch or feeling.

Tonic Labyrinthine Reflex (TLR)—A reflex stimulated by the position of the head in space and the position of the body, specifically prone (on the stomach) or supine (on the back). When in the prone position, the body will remain in a flexed, curled position. When in the supine position, the body will be dominated by extension (or straightening).

Vestibular—Pertaining to the functions of the inner ear dealing with posture, equilibrium, muscular tones and orientation in environmental space.

Vision—The result of the student's ability to interpret and understand the information that comes to the student through her eyes.

Visual Efficiency—Refers to a group of visual skills important for success, including eye teaming, eye movement and eye focusing speed and accuracy.

Visual Perception—Refers to a group of visual skills which help us interpret visual information from our surroundings.

Visualization—The ability to create pictures in our minds eye based on what is known.

Index

Index

About A Chance To Grow 117
Alligator Crawl..47
All Through The Day 89
Appendices 113
Awesome Autumn Theme.................104

Balance and Vestibular Activities 31
Balance Beam..40
Basic Vision..82
Bugs Bugs Bugs Theme......................110

Center Time Activities 91
Circle Time Activities 90
CORE Vision Activities 61
Cross Patterning 59

Driver's Ed 70

Eye Movement Activities 63

Fabulous Food Theme........................106
Flamingos...39
Flower Power 66
Focusing Activities 81
Free Creep 55

Glossary... 131
Gross Motor Activities 45
Gross Motor Time Activities 90

Helicopter Spins 35
Hopscotch..42

Introduction 8

Letter to Your Families 115
Loop de Loos 76

Magic Erasers...72
Movement and Learning 19

Near/Far Focus 84

Overhead Ladder 57
Overs and Unders 78
Overview of Activities............................21

Pencil Rolls..33
Popcorn 27
Putting It All Together............................87

Rebounder 44
Reflex Activities......................................23

Slap Track..50
Slap Track Pocket Ideas.......................53
S.M.A.R.T. Courses 93
S.M.A.R.T. – E.C. Project 121
S.M.A.R.T. Pre-K 13
S.M.A.R.T. Pre-K Guide Roadmap........22
S.M.A.R.T. Themes.............................103
Stable Table..37
Superman 25
Swinging Ball..68

Tactile Trackers 64
Things That Go Theme 108
Thumbs Up 74
Transition Activities............................... 90

Understanding S.M.A.R.T. Principles 11

136 • S.M.A.R.T. Pre-K CORE Program Guide © 2011, A Chance To Grow, Inc.

Made in the USA
San Bernardino, CA
31 October 2016